THE
COUNTRY WESTERN
GUIDE TO LIFE

MICKEY FLODIN & CAROL FLODIN

CB

CONTEMPORARY
BOOKS

CHICAGO

*To our mamas . . . who sang us our first
country songs*

◆

*To all who gave friendly help and valuable advice
during the roundup of this book, we say,
"Thanks, pardners."*

Photo credits:
Dick Patrick: 3, 14 (top), 15 (bottom left), 16 (top and bottom left), 17 (top left and right, and bottom left), 18 (top), 19 (glitz hat and girl with hat), 20 (right top and bottom), 23 (bottom two), 24 (center right); Professional Rodeo Cowboys Association: 4 (center right), 68, 72 (center); DMI: Kevin Winter: 4, 18 (top), 74, 76 (bottom), 77, 78, 82; Alex Oliveira: 75, 76 (top); S. Dakota Tourism: 26; Rick Norman: 28; Western Custom: 36 (top left); Yippy Yi Yea: 36 (top right); Doolings of Santa Fe: 36 (bottom left); Image Photography: Billie Garner: 36 (center); Copper Star Cattle & Trading Co: 36 (bottom right); Collections by Otis: 37 (top and center); Crystal Farm Antler Chandeliers: 37 (bottom left); M. C. Limited: 37 (bottom right); Curly Leiker: 39 (center left); Archive Photos: 52, 54, 92, 121, 122; East Moreno Ranch: 58; Hake's Americana & Collectibles: 61 (bottom); The Dude Ranchers' Association: 72 (top); Texas A&M University: 72 (bottom); Collect-A-Card: 88, 89, 90, 106, (right); Country Music Hall of Fame: 93; Country Music Association: 94, 95; Silver Dollar City: 100 (top), 102 (top); Branson Chamber of Commerce: 101 (top), 126 (top); Moe Bandy Americana Theatre: 102 (center); Donnie Beauchamp: 103, 104, (bottom); Opryland Public Relations: 104 (top); National Bit, Spur & Saddle Collectors Association: 61 (top right, center right, and bottom right), 120; Adventures in Cassettes: 123; Jim Owens & Associates, Inc: 124.

Illustrations, photography (unless otherwise noted), and book design by Mickey Flodin

Published by Contemporary Books, Inc.

Two Prudential Plaza, Chicago, Illinois 60601-6790

Manufactured in the United States of America

International Standard Book Number: 0-8092-3776-8

10   9   8   7   6   5   4   3   2   1

CONTENTS

Chapter 3   The Right Lingo   45

Chapter 4   The Cowboy ... America's Hero   51

Chapter 5   It's in the Music   73

Chapter 6   The Music Makes Them Sing   87

Chapter 7 Where to Find the Music 99

Chapter 8 Cookin' with Country Stars 107

Chapter 9 Entertainment 113

Index 127

Howdy!

Country music and the western fever have hit the nation from coast to coast, and it's the biggest roundup ever. Everyone, young and old, is pulling on their cowboy boots and discovering the New West. Even college kids, who once danced to their favorite rock groups, are kicking up their heels to "Boot Scootin' Boogie" and other hot country tracks. "Country music is sweeping the world like a tidal wave and it truly is the sound of the nineties," says Lorianne Crook of TNN's (The Nashville Network) "Crook and Chase." Bet your boots that country music and the western lifestyle is in—it's chic, cool, and downright fun.

You could say we are being hit with a country western renewal. Dance floors are switching from rock 'n' roll to do-si-do. Giant department stores are stocking western wear—shirts, pants and accessories—to dude up in. Radio stations by the hundreds have changed to hot country music, while TV can't get enough of country stars such as Garth Brooks, Clint Black, Vince Gill, George Strait, Reba McEntire, Pam Tillis, Trisha Yearwood—the list is endless.

Could it be that America is longing for

a simpler time, longing to return to its roots and a less complicated way of living? Has the lightning-paced, microchip information age of the last decade caused us to search out our past and a bit of the Old West? Perhaps Dolly Parton said it best when Jay Leno asked her why country music is so popular: "I think," said Dolly, "that when cowboy movies, westerns, went off the air . . . that people kinda missed the cowboy and . . . that it's a simple way to get back to basics. Plus . . . the kids, the new country now . . . they love the dress . . . they love those boots . . . those jeans and those hats."

It's anyone's guess why, but country music and the western lifestyle have struck a chord in the hearts of Americans. The powerful lyrics are truthful and down-home. The clothes are fun, functional, fashionable, and have people hankering for more. One thing is certain, this cosmo-country roundup is taking over not only America but the entire planet.

This book is your guide as you hit the country western trail. "Happy trails," partner.

Hang up
your saddle
and
stay a spell.

Chapter 1

DUDIN' UP WESTERN

Pure Country Western Quiz

How much do you know about country music and the western lifestyle? Take this quiz to find out. Remember, your score will be announced on the Grand Ole Opry in Nashville.

1. From what region of the U.S. did country music and the western lifestyle emerge?
   A. From the southern and western U.S.
   B. From Brooklyn, New York
   C. From a volcano
2. Nashville's nickname, besides "Music City USA," is _____?
   A. "Hillbilly Heaven"
   B. "City of Neon Cowboys"
   C. "Athens of the South"
3. What really is the "Nashville Sound"?
   A. The sound of traffic
   B. Country-pop fusion
   C. The sound of money
4. Who is TNN's most famous talk show host?
   A. Jay Leno
   B. Ralph Emery
   C. Rush Limbaugh
5. Who is Shotgun Red?
   A. A bubble gum
   B. A cowboy with sore eyes
   C. A popular cowboy puppet on TNN
6. Branson, Missouri, is especially known for being _____.
   A. The Country Music Show Capital of America
   B. A small dot on the U.S. map
   C. A hillbilly's paradise
7. What historic building became the home of the Grand Ole Opry from 1943 to 1974 and became known as "the mother church of country music"?
   A. The White House
   B. The Ryman Auditorium
   C. The Hermitage
8. Which dance did former President Reagan declare to be the national folk dance of the U.S.?
   A. The twist
   B. The bunny hop
   C. The square dance
9. What best describes a cowpoke?
   A. A cowboy who is slow
   B. A cowboy who loses his temper while working with cattle
   C. A cowboy who works with cattle
10. What's the name of a popular country singer who won the PRCA's world championship bareback riding title in 1976?
    A. Ross Perot
    B. Chris LeDoux
    C. Dan Rather
11. The Grand Ole Opry is radio's longest-running regularly scheduled show. What are the call letters of the Nashville radio station that airs the program?
    A. TWA
    B. WSM
    C. BVD
12. Who was Louis L'Amour?
    A. A famous chef from France
    B. A famous science-fiction writer
    C. A famous western novelist
13. What is the symbol of the Professional Rodeo Cowboy Association (PRCA)?
    A. The mechanical bull
    B. The donkey
    C. The saddle bronc rider
14. What is the defining characteristic of the western shirt?
    A. A monogramed armadillo
    B. The scalloped yolk on the back of the shirt
    C. Underarm B.O.
15. Who starred in *Pure Country*?
    A. George Washington

B. George Strait
C. George Lucas

16. In square dancing, "yellowrock" means _____?
   A. A friendly hug
   B. A nickname for the caller
   C. You're going in the wrong direction

17. What musical instrument was most favored by rural folk and for many years was considered the defining instrument of country music?
   A. The saxophone
   B. The kazoo
   C. The fiddle

18. How high should cowboy boots be?
   A. Up to the crotch
   B. No set height—if the boots fit, wear them
   C. High enough to keep the rattlesnakes out

19. "Kicker" is a term used to describe what?
   A. Soccer shoes
   B. The way to check a tire on a pickup truck
   C. Cowboy or cowgirl dancers

20. A country music song usually tells a _____.
   A. lie
   B. joke
   C. story

21. In a country song, what is the most important element?
   A. The music
   B. The beat
   C. The lyrics

22. What does CMA stand for?
   A. Country Mecca Awards
   B. Country Music Appetite
   C. Country Music Association

23. What does WPRA stand for?
   A. The call letters of a Cincinnati radio station
   B. Wild Possum Roundup Association
   C. Women's Professional Rodeo Association

24. Who is a true national hero of American culture?
   A. Garfield
   B. The cowboy
   C. Captain Kirk of the USS *Enterprise*

25. What is the name of the California based organization with the initials ACM?
   A. A Country Mile
   B. Academy of Country Music
   C. A Cowboy Mystique

26. In country western dancing, what does "buckle polishing" mean?
   A. To spitshine your buckle
   B. Fighting over a cowgirl
   C. Slow dancing

27. The highest honor bestowed upon a country performer by the Country Music Association is the award for _____.
   A. Hillbilly of the Year
   B. Entertainer of the Year
   C. Ham of the Year

Will Your Score Make Your Spurs Jangle?

25–27 correct: You're pure country. You were country before it was cool to be country.
21–24 correct: You're on your way to being pure country.
16–20 correct: You're straddling the fence. Ouch!
10–15 correct: You're on the fringe of country but still missing its benefits.
0–9 correct: You need this book—and your score graded on a curve.

Answers: 1. A; 2. C; 3. B; 4. B; 5. C; 6. A; 7. B; 8. C; 9. C; 10. B; 11. B; 12. C; 13. C; 14. B; 15. B; 16. A; 17. C; 18. B; 19. C; 20. C; 21. C; 22. C; 23. C; 24. B; 25. B; 26. C; 27. B

11

The Cowboy

He has the personality of a maverick good ol' boy and wears a hat and boots.

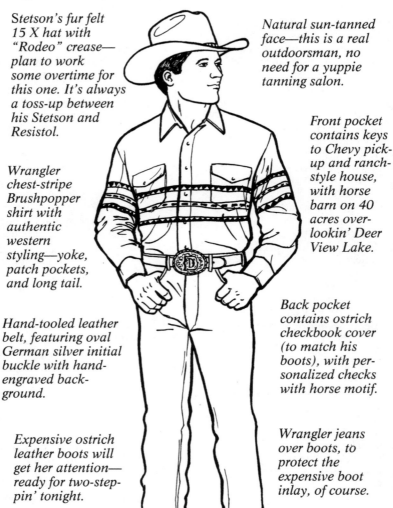

Stetson's fur felt 15 X hat with "Rodeo" crease— plan to work some overtime for this one. It's always a toss-up between his Stetson and Resistol.

Wrangler chest-stripe Brushpopper shirt with authentic western styling—yoke, patch pockets, and long tail.

Hand-tooled leather belt, featuring oval German silver initial buckle with hand-engraved background.

Expensive ostrich leather boots will get her attention— ready for two-steppin' tonight.

Natural sun-tanned face—this is a real outdoorsman, no need for a yuppie tanning salon.

Front pocket contains keys to Chevy pick-up and ranch-style house, with horse barn on 40 acres over-lookin' Deer View Lake.

Back pocket contains ostrich checkbook cover (to match his boots), with per-sonalized checks with horse motif.

Wrangler jeans over boots, to protect the expensive boot inlay, of course.

The Cowgirl

The reason a cowboy takes a bath and learns the two-step.

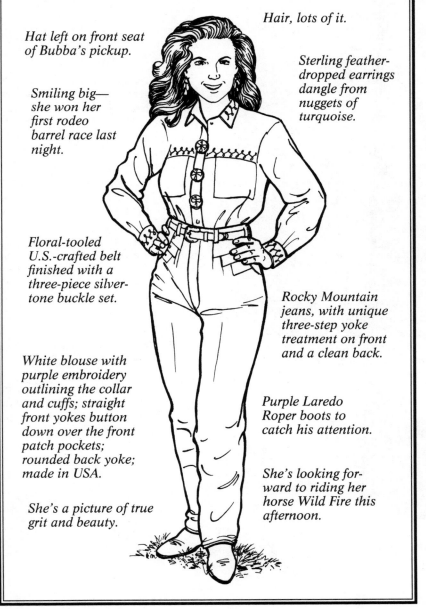

Hair, lots of it.

Hat left on front seat of Bubba's pickup.

Sterling feather-dropped earrings dangle from nuggets of turquoise.

Smiling big— she won her first rodeo barrel race last night.

Floral-tooled U.S.-crafted belt finished with a three-piece silver-tone buckle set.

Rocky Mountain jeans, with unique three-step yoke treatment on front and a clean back.

White blouse with purple embroidery outlining the collar and cuffs; straight front yokes button down over the front patch pockets; rounded back yoke; made in USA.

Purple Laredo Roper boots to catch his attention.

She's looking for- ward to riding her horse Wild Fire this afternoon.

She's a picture of true grit and beauty.

Ropin' the Western Look: The Clothes to Wear

The look of the West is more than fun and trendy, it's durable and practical. It's the look of the independent, pioneering spirit that conquered the harsh, rugged elements of the West. Dressing western is dressing American.

The work clothes of the Wild West have become the fashion statement of today. There are five essential pieces needed to corral today's dynamite western look: boots, a hat, a shirt, jeans, and a belt with a buckle. These simple basics can transform any wannabe into a western sharpshooter. It's a style that will do you proud. Once transformed, you live the fantasy, you become the cowboy or the cowgirl riding the open range looking for the new frontier.

Not just any jean will do for the western look. Western jeans are different from mainstream jeans—they were made for the working cowboy and his unique

Bronco with crop top by Circle T, fringe trim, and Roughrider jeans give a Wild West look.

Shirt and jeans make life comfortable.

Western jackets are bold and strong.

Southwestern designs say it all.

Stripes are a western classic.

Man's geometric-style shirt

Man's Aztec-style shirt

The typical female western-jeans buyer has 10–25 pairs of jeans in her closet.

The basic western look

Button snaps give the look of chaps to these jeans; the blouse is full of romance with its flutter cape design.

Did Ya Know?

The western yoke was originally created by the cowboy cutting off his shirttail and sewing it on the back and shoulders of his shirt, adding extra protection from the elements. Today, it's the defining characteristic of the western shirt and a great area for creative designs.

A year-round favorite, the linen blend sport coat; a western straw hat tops it off.

needs. They have five pockets; the fifth is a watch pocket made deep enough so a rider doesn't lose his prized watch at full gallop. The inseam is longer, allowing the leg bottom to reach the bottom of the boot when in the saddle. The leg bottom opening fits snugly over a western boot. The back pockets are high so a rider doesn't sit on his wallet, saving him from a walletectomy later on. The rise is higher to keep from binding at the waist, and the back is higher to keep the shirttail tucked in. These jeans have more seat and thigh room, for freedom of movement, and a zipper fly to make dressing easier.

Today, western jeans are alive with a rainbow of colors and ever-changing styles—a tribute to the functional, timeless design of cowboy jeans. For that authentic western look, no question about it, the five-pocket style is number one, but there are other 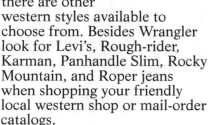 western styles available to choose from. Besides Wrangler look for Levi's, Rough-rider, Karman, Panhandle Slim, Rocky Mountain, and Roper jeans when shopping your friendly local western shop or mail-order catalogs.

The western shirt was originally designed as a no-frills work

This fringe outfit is ready for two-steppin'.

shirt. But, with the emergence of the Wild West shows, Roy Rogers and Dale Evans, and the rodeo, satin shirts with fancy fringes and decorative yokes began showing up. Today's styles range from basic everyday wear to fancy clothes for opening night at the rodeo.

ztec-design
irts—a
ust in a
estern
ardrobe.

Stirrup-stretch denim jeans always look good with boots; put on an attitude with the "Cassidy" black leather hat with a concho hat band.

Did Ya Know?

During the Old West days the vest became a popular garment for the cowboys, since few shirts had pockets. Also, the work season was too warm for coats, so the cowboy wore a vest because it had several pockets to carry items in. Nowadays, these items usually get thrown on the dashboard of the pickup truck.

For a classy/casual look, wear with a pair of jeans.

The Western Hat

No good cowboy would ever be without his hat. Considered an essential part of cowboy dress, its brim provided shade on hot summer days. The cowboy's hat was also used to fan his campfire, to draw water for his horse, or used as a flyswatter, a pillow, or a horsewhip. The Old West cowboy would pay from two to six months' wages for a hat, which often lost its shape after a few wearings.

While vacationing in the Midwest in the 1850s, Philadelphia hatmaker John B. Stetson realized that the cowboy needed a bigger hat to protect him from the elements. Inspired, he created the "Boss of the Plains"—a wide-brimmed hat of quality felt. This new hat kept its shape in rain, snow, and wind, and the high crown kept the head cool. The 10-gallon cowboy hat was born, and Stetson was ridin' tall . . . all the way to the bank.

Today's western hats come in three types: straw, fur felt, and 100 percent wool felt. All come in many styles and shapes. Straw hats are rated on a "star" system and fur felt hats on an "X" system—the more stars or Xs the higher the quality.

With western fashion thundering across America today, it doesn't matter if you're an urban cowboy or cowgirl or one who works the range, there's a style for everyone. Go ahead. Live the legend.

George Strait in his Resistol hat.

Thunder Rolls "Garth Brooks"

Quarter Horse

Big Spender

Silverstreak

Rodeo

Glitz

Charlie Horse 1 with Critter Parts

Riverboat "Tanya Tucker"

Cattleman

Bangora

Western Hat Care 101

1. Don't wrap your hat in plastic. It holds in heat.
2. Don't set your hat down on its brim—the circular part that surrounds the crown's base like a doughnut. It will lose its shape.
3. Don't handle your hat by its brim.

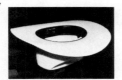

Handle it gently by the crown— the round, top part of the hat that sits on the brim.
4. Set your hat down on its crown only.
5. Brush your hat before storing in a hat case.
6. Follow the adage: "It's the cowboy way—straw from Memorial to Labor Day."
7. Purchase a hat caddy for your pick-up so that your dog doesn't eat your hat for lunch.

Did Ya Know?

In the Old West, cowboys could tell what part of the country another cowboy came from by the crease in his hat.

You can only have a fine-looking hat by getting a custom hand-shaping and crease. Western shops and mail-order companies will do the job for you. Don't be tempted to whack it with your hand. Never.

Popular Crease Names:
Nightrider, J-Boy, Alpine, The Hand, Cutter, Bronc, Horseshoe, Rancher, Frontier, Gunslinger, Roper, Tycoon, and Top Hand.

Steppin' Tall: Western Boots

Western boots, in a variety of styles, are bustin' out all over the cosmo-cowboy fashion landscape like a wild bronc out of the chute. There are dozens of designs with varied colors and textures to quench anyone's thirst for style and comfort in western footwear. No matter what your needs, whether it be horseback riding, two-steppin', working, hiking, dressing up, or just spectating, there's a western boot to fit your lifestyle. They are being seen from the barn to the boardroom. And the array of exotic leathers—lizard, snake, alligator, and ostrich—make "boot hunting" all the more fun.

Cowboy boots were designed not only for comfort, but for the cowboy's safety as well. The boot shaft protects the ankle and lower leg from chafing while riding. The pointed toes make it easier for the rider to find the stirrups, while the high heels hold the boots more securely in the stirrups. The tops are loose enough so the rider, when thrown from his horse, can quickly slide out of a boot if it gets caught in the stirrup.

Though a certain amount of neglect can give boots an "authentic" look, experts agree that clean boots lead to longevity. Tips to keep in mind:
• Dust and dirt act as sandpaper, rubbing the natural grooves and causing cracks. After each wearing, wipe your boots with a soft rag.
• Never dry boots near heat, such as a fireplace. Dry them at room temperature.
• Natural oils keep leather soft and supple, so condition your boots to seal in and preserve the oils.
• Polish your boots when needed.
• Waterproof your western boots before rain and snow arrive.

Did Ya Know?

When heels first were worn, they were only worn by men of nobility. During the Middle Ages, with so much waste on the ground, the high heels offered some protection. From this we get the expression "well-heeled." The cowboy boot is definitely loaded with nobility.

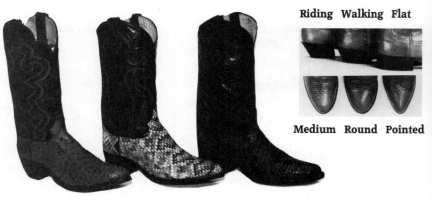

Riding Walking Flat

Medium Round Pointed

Ostrich   Rattlesnake   Red Lizard

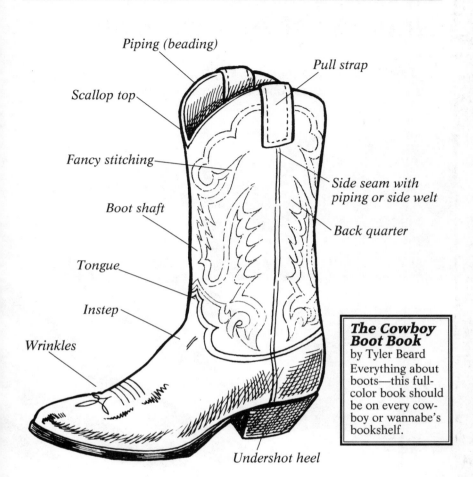

Piping (beading)

Pull strap

Scallop top

Fancy stitching

Boot shaft

Tongue

Instep

Wrinkles

Side seam with piping or side welt

Back quarter

Undershot heel

The Cowboy Boot Book
by Tyler Beard
Everything about boots—this full-color book should be on every cowboy or wannabe's bookshelf.

Fringe boot   Lizard   Hot "retro" boots bring back the western-movie era of the 1930s through the 1950s.   Rugged outback

New West Accessories

Great-looking gear added to your western wardrobe can make you stand out on the new wild frontier.

Ornately engraved buckles can be as tough and as big as the West.

Boot bracelets on Roper-style boots look great.

Leather belts, with western motifs, add the right touch.

Add a colorful finish to a western hat with a hat band—leather, horsehair, and silver concho are good choices.

Did Ya Know?

The love of horses is evident in western accessories. The "concho" is adapted from ancient horse ornaments brought to this country by the conquistadors.

There's always a good purse to take to the next rodeo.

Attractive earrings and big bracelets will set you apart—silver, beads, and natural stones are as timeless as the West itself.

For those who don't wear spurs, consider collecting them instead—there's a stampede of buyers who will pay thousands of dollars for the old, rare ones.

Bolo ties for all occasions—why waste time making a perfect knot?

Bandanas, the wild, wild rags of the West—in bold colors to choose from—can be used as scarves or headbands.

eep in time with the West.

Little Buckaroos & Buckarettes

Cody at "Krazy Horse Ranch" in Branson, where you can enjoy chuckwagon cookouts, horseback riding, and even a train ride (417-334-5068). It's only a stone's throw from Wayne Newton's theater.

An authentic replica of the Old West covered wagon.

Kids love to dude up western in jeans, hat, boots, shirt, and belt.

Ruffled skirt and blouse with hat and boots, for a real hoedown style.

Pete the Potty Pony makes potty training fun, western style.

Did Ya Know?

The cowboy wore chaps (pronounced "shaps") to protect his legs from thorny vegetation and the elements. *Chaparreras*, Spanish for "leather britches," and later shortened by the cowboy to "chaps," were an idea adopted by Texans from their Mexican neighbors. By the late 1860s and early 1870s, the "shotgun" pattern was being used—leggings with the seat cut out, large front pockets, and fringes on the side seams. For the working cowboy today, chaps are still an important part of the gear. They add an extra touch of the Old West for the rodeo cowboy as well.

The Bandana

The bandana is an important accessory for the cowboy, more than just something to "sneeze at." It has many practical purposes, such as: for a tourniquet, bandage, or sling; for a bronc blind; for protecting the face from dust and cold; for a pot holder; and more. Here are some ways to use that "wild rag" today even if you're not on the range:

• To summon help when in distress (if you get hit by a Mack truck!)
• To use as a cat or dog collar
• As a neck scarf
• As an all-purpose napkin
• For dusting the house
• To check the truck's oil
• As a western belt for the ladies
• As designer baby hippins (diapers): just cover the buckaroo's pampers with a bandana.
• As a western babushka
• As a headband while working out or jogging
• As a washcloth when desperate.

• As a pollution-control mask (be sure not to wear this look to the bank)

• To wrap a sandwich for lunch

• And for the most important reason—to get a cowgirl's attention

Western Festivals to Wear Your Duds To

Cheyenne Frontier Days
P.O. Box 2477
Cheyenne, WY 82003
(307) 778-7200
(800) 227-6336
Chuckwagon races, parades, top country stars performing. "The daddy of 'em all." July.

Cowboy Poetry Gathering
Western Folklife Center
501 Railroad St.
Elko, NV 89801
(702) 738-7508
(800) 748-4466
The biggest annual roundup of cowboy poets. A great western catalog available. January.

Custer State Park Buffalo Roundup
Custer, South Dakota
(800) 732-5682
Bring your camera and see a real buffalo roundup in the beautiful Black Hills. October.

Michael Martin Murphey's West Fest
Copper Mountain, CO 80443
(303) 968-2882
A three-day festival giving tribute to the West. Music, art, and native culture. September.

Nebraskaland Days
208 E. 3rd
North Platte, NE 69103
(308) 532-7939 Family fun with a rodeo, parade, dancing, and frontier history. June.

Omak Stampede and Suicide Race
Omak, WA 09941
(800) 933-6625
Where you can see the most famous horseback mountain race in the world plus dancing, music, and a rodeo. August.

Pendleton Roundup
P.O. Box 609
Pendleton, OR 97801
(800) 524-2984
Westward Ho is "The Fastest Moving Rodeo in America!" Cowboy breakfast, dancing, and fun. September.

Tom Mix Roundup
Driftwood, PA 15832
(814) 546-2628
Celebrating the memory of the great cowboy. Parade, food, and music. July.

Tyler County Dogwood Festival
507 N. Pine
Woodville, TX 75979
(409) 283-2632
"Western Weekend" inclues a Wild West rodeo, western dancing, and a parade featuring more than 1,800 riders with wagons, buggies, and oxen. March.

Wild West Days
Grants, NM 87020
(505) 287-4802
Country music and a rodeo, arts and crafts fair, and a chili cook-off. July.

XIT Rodeo and Reunion
Dalhart Chamber of Commerce
P.O. Box 967
Dalhart, TX 79022
(806) 249-5646
"The largest range in the world under fence." Rodeo, parade, dance, antique car show, and top country stars entertaining. August.

Did Ya Know?

During the gold rush of the 1850s, Levi Strauss, a German immigrant, went west thinking the miners would need tents. Upon arriving he discovered they needed tough pants to work in instead. Making and supplying miners with canvas pants, he struck "gold." Before Levi came to their rescue, the miners could wear out a pair of pants in three weeks. Later, the cowboys took a liking to these sturdy, copper-riveted, reinforced jeans because they could take the punishment of range and ranch work. As time went on, the indigo-blue Levi's became synonymous with the cowboy and the Old West.

The Suburban Cowboy's Dress Rules

• Don't be afraid to get your boots dirty. Only "drugstore" cowboys keep their boots perfect at all times.

• Don't use your bandana to blow your nose in the same day you plan to wear it around your neck.

• Don't squat with your spurs on.

• Don't forget to spit-shine your belt buckle at least once a week.

• Don't ever wear chaps without jeans underneath.

• Don't wear shirts without the western yoke, and this doesn't mean getting "sunnyside up" on your shirt in the morning.

• Don't use spurs for brass knuckles.

• Don't sleep in your waterbed with your spurs on.

• Don't wear spurs on your Reeboks.

• Don't ever wear a belt buckle that weighs less than five pounds.

• Don't let your cowboy hat get out of shape or lose its crease. You don't want to send mixed messages.

Where to Get the Western Look: Mail-Order Shopping

Buying from the best in the West will help you to dude up right for the '90s. Wearing the wild frontier look is easy, relaxing, and fun. These full-color catalogs will bring the romance of the Wild West to your homestead.

Boot Town
10838 N. Central
Dallas, TX 75231
(800) 222-6687

Cheyenne Outfitters
P.O. Box 12013
Cheyenne, WY 82003
(800) 234-0432

Drysdales, Inc.
1555 N. 107th East Ave.
Tulsa, OK 74116
(800) 444-6481

Justin Discount Boots & Cowboy Outfitters
P.O. Box 67
Justin, TX 76247
(800) 677-2668

Luskey's Western Stores
101 N. Houston St.
Fort Worth, TX 76102
(800) 752-7081

Rod's Western Palace
3099 Silver Dr.
Columbus, OH 43223
(800) 325-8508

Roeme R's
1920 N. Broadway
Santa Maria, CA 93454
(800) 242-1890

PFI   2816 S. INGRAM MILL ROAD
SPRINGFIELD, MO, 65809

Clothing, boots, and accessories in this chapter are supplied by PFI, "Missouri's Largest Western Store." When visiting Branson, stop by and see their new store just off U.S. Highway 65 and Battlefield Road in Springfield. It's 30,000 square feet of shopping fun. Free catalog (800) 284-8191.

Sheplers
P.O. Box 7702
Wichita, KS 67277
(800) 835-4004

Soda Creek Western Outfitters
355 Lincoln Ave.
Steamboat Springs, CO 80477
(800) 824-8426

Tonto Rim Times
P.O. Box 463
Salem, IN 47167
(800) 242-4287

Miller Stockman
P.O. Box 5127
Denver, CO 80217
(800) 688-9888

Custom Boots

These boot makers have designed boots for presidents, movie stars, and your favorite country music stars.

Ammons
9401 Carnegie
El Paso, TX 79925
(915) 595-2100

Little's Boot Company
110 Division
San Antonio, TX 78214
(512) 923-2221
Custom boot makers since 1915.

Custom Hats & Hat Renovation

Catalena Hatters
203 N. Main
Bryan, TX 77803
(409) 822-4423

Did Ya Know?

If you are looking for something unusual, something not found on the "rack," Manuel (who has a store in Nashville) can make it for you. He's been a "costume designer" to the brightest stars in Hollywood, Nashville, and Las Vegas for many years, making one-of-a-kind designer outfits. His wardrobe designs have appeared in such movies and TV shows as *Urban Cowboy*, "Bonanza," "The Big Valley," and "McCloud." Manuel has designed clothes for Randy Travis, Dwight Yoakam, Marty Stuart, Loretta Lynn, Glen Campbell, Travis Tritt, and Dolly Parton, to name a few. But be sure to bring a big bankroll, for Manuel's services don't come cheap: a suit can cost $10,000.

Chapter 2

A DOWN-HOME
LIFESTYLE

Choosing a Handle

Now that you have the western look, you need the right nickname or handle to go with your new style. During the Old West days a cowboy was known by his nickname—without it, the cowboy was like a bull without horns. Because it was impolite to ask a stranger his full name, handles or nicknames became popular during this period. Handles usually related to a person's looks, actions, or the place where he made a reputation. So, why not grab a handle for yourself? The only rule is to be colorful, descriptive, and never boring.

Cowboy Nicknames

Animal names are great for the outdoor type, or maybe you've been called an "animal" before. Either way there's a name here for you.

Bear For that good ol' boy who loves to hug.
Beaver Cheeks The cowboy who is never to busy to smile at the ladies.
Catfish The cowboy with a waxed mustache.
Chigger The guy who gets under people's skin.
Crawdad This is great for the man who shuns responsibilities. One out of two men should be able to wear this one.
Frog Any cowboy with a hoarse sounding voice.
Gator For any lawyer who wears a cowboy hat.
Moo For the real cowpoke.
Owlhead For the cowboy who always has a wisecrack.
Possum The guy who has a constant grin, especially for the ladies.
Snake The "reptile" who has a habit of sneaking out on his lady deserves this one.
Turtle For a slow-movin' cowboy.

Country Hunk Nicknames

The country hunk is usually tall and handsome, but don't despair if you're neither. It's the image you need to project, and country has all the props. Even if you're short, boots will add inches to your stature. If you're *very* short, the "hat act" works every time. How else can six to eight inches of instant growth take place without major surgery, pain, or hormone shots?

Bandana For the pumping-iron type who thinks that bandanas are used by real cowboys only to wipe the sweat off their faces.

Bronco For the cowboy no cowgirl has ever been able to tame.

Chaps For the man whose hairy legs look like a cowboy's wooly chaps.

Gunslinger A real desperado.

Lonestar This man likes to contemplate. Like the cowboys of old he believes that if you don't have nothin' to say, you just don't.

Maverick For the man who measures his manhood by the amount of freedom and independence he has.

Rifleman This man usually has a pickup truck with a rifle in the back window and a bumper sticker that says "Support the NRA—Good Guys Need Guns Too."

Rodeo Man For the daring man that can't buy life insurance.

Tractor For that big man, *real* big.

Using Initials

Two initials instead of a first name gives anyone wearing a hat and boots authenticity. Don't worry, most people won't even ask you what the initials stand for. Try these on for size: **J.R., B.J., J.T., R.T.,** or **L.J.**

Combining initials with a nickname can be quite effective, for instance, J. R. "Catfish" Carter.

"Old-Timey Grub" Nicknames

Most country men are from the "hard lard and gravy" section of the United States and love old-timey food. A food nickname is a natural for them, especially since most cowboys can't hear the words "chuck wagon" without salivating. Here are a few "grub" nicknames:

Bone Head	**Gumbo**
Chilihead	**Pork Chop**
Corn Bread	**Potluck**
Fritter	**Stringbean**
Gator Tail	**T-Bone**

Popular Old West Nicknames if Your Name Was Bill

Big Foot Bill
Bill of the Lazy A Outfit
Billy the Kid
Buffalo Bill
Flat-Nosed Bill
Long Bill
Pecos Bill
Texas Bill
Tinker Bill
Wild Bill

Cowgirl Nicknames

For the down-home country image, try some grub-influenced nicknames. Warning: use with CAUTION. If you're not the domestic type, stay clear of any nicknames that could incriminate you. These names will send the message to any country hunk that you can "grow it, can it, and cook it" just like his mama did.

Dixie For the country girl who knows what's cookin'.
Gumbo Cha-Cha For the country girl that's spicy.
Honey Dew For the country girl who can "dew" it all.
Ladyfish Every crawdaddie needs a ladyfish.
Peaches For that naturally sweet cowgirl.

Sweet Nibbles For the girl who believes everything that's whispered in her ear.
Sweet Pea Even if you have to fake it, be sweet if you use this one. Don't use on PMS days.
Sweet Potato If your man is a "country ham," you need a nickname that goes well with his.

Here are some names that you only use for the darlin' of your life: **Honey Bun, Punkin', Sugar Foot, Sugar Lips, Sweet'art, Sweetie Pie.**

Cowgirl Middle Names

A country girl should always have a middle name. If you don't have one, don't hesitate to borrow one. Some middle names are: Lee, Sue, Faye, Lou, Anna, Mae, and Jean. Some good combinations are: Peggy Sue, Mary Lou, Billy Jean, Anna Lee, Ella Mae. When you say your new middle name, add a little twang for authenticity.

Cowgirl Nicknames of the Old West

The cowgirl of the Old West was a combination of true grit and beauty. She had the guts of a man, the patience of a woman. She never had to prove she was equal with the cowboy. She always received equal work and equal pay: wind, sweat, and dirt. She is one of the reasons the West was won. Here are some nicknames she wore in the Old West:

Bulldog Kate
Calamity Jane
Cattle Kate
Cattle Queen
Cowgirl Cutie
Hurricane Nell
Lady Boss
Lady Gunslinger
Prairie Rose
Queenie
Rattlesnake Ann
Sage Hen
Shorthorn
Wild Rose

Pet Names Go Country

Now that you have a handle, here are some good struttin' names for your pets.

Cats

Bait The cat that has fish breath.

Barbecue A black cat who loves the outdoors.

Biscuit This one shows up for breakfast whenever country biscuits and gravy are served.

Casserole For the cat that's pleasingly plump.

Country Hunk This male cat has it all. He's the cat's meow.

Hootin' A country cat that loves to have fun.

Jukebox The cat who never stops purrin'.

Opry This cat is a class act—like those who appear on the Grand Ole Opry.

Patsy The cat that falls to pieces easily. Name her after country singer Patsy Cline, whose song "I Fall to Pieces" became a number-one hit in 1961.

Reba The lovely cat who has a powerful meow.

Rockabilly This cat is a little bit country and a little bit rock 'n' roll.

Trisha If you love the way your cat meows, name her after country singer Trisha Yearwood.

Dogs

Bull For the yard dog that you don't want to upset.

Chuck Wagon This dog is always looking for something to eat.

Fox For any red dog.

Grub With this dog there is no need for a garbage disposal in your kitchen.

Gunsmoke Any dog that has more bark than bite.

Otis Name him after Travis Tritt's beagle.

Rio For the ranch dog who lives in the Southwest.

Rowdy For the dog that is constantly barking.

Shotgun The dog that loves to go huntin' with you.

Tejas An Indian word that means "friends."

Tush For that lazy dog.

Vapor For the dog who embarrasses you when company comes over. (*Vapor* is an old southern word that means "gas.")

Wild Bill Name him after Wild Bill Hickok, the lawman of the Old West.

Horses

Diamond Rio Any horse that has a diamond shape on its forehead—named after the country group.

Dolly This horse is beautiful and full of country charm.

Garth The horse that is pure energy.

Goldrush For the horse that is golden in color.

Jamboree A friendly country horse.

Kicker This horse makes all the right moves, like a country western dancer.

Lady Boss You would never ride this horse bareback.

Lady Hawk This horse never misses the chance to make you feel like you're flying.

Stampede The horse that moves like greased lightning.

Strait If your horse makes you feel like pure country, name him after George Strait.

Sundance A smooth-moving horse.

Travis After the country singer Randy Travis, who loves horses.

The Wild West Family Room

The Wild West roundup is changing the way Americans decorate. To corral this western look, combine a variety of textures. Coarse woven fabrics look great with glassy pottery. Leather, with its smooth suppleness, always gives a room a feeling of the outdoors. Throw a colorful Indian blanket on the sofa for added appeal. Accessorize with authentic and reproduced western art and artifacts. This frontier look can be found by hitting your local department stores and specialty shops. For the collector's items and the unusual, like old western gear, don't forget flea markets, antique shops, used furniture stores, and those whoop-and-holler garage sales. This current stampede for the western lifestyle is driven by an ardent romance with the past. With a little touch of the frontier, anyone can experience their own home on the range.

1. Horseshoe floor lamp. Made from horseshoes from J.R.'s ranch.
2. Ottoman with real cowhide. Gives the secure feeling of Elsie the cow being nearby.
3. Furniture should be large and comfortable, for Ponderosa-sized relatives and their rowdy kids.
4. The five-pound bass that didn't get away.
5. Magazines on coffee table: *Country America, Western Horseman, Field and Stream,* and *Southwest Art.*

6. Coffee table made with a slab of rock and ponderosa pine for a solid, rugged look. Every cowboy needs a place to hang his feet.

7. Local paper, with stockyard report, and cup of black coffee—the cowboy never could understand why anyone would put milk in coffee.

8. Longhorn rack that family bought while visiting relatives in Texas. Don't ask about the "vacation."

9. Collector's gun. Bubba loves it when huntin' conversations come up. He has stories to share with anyone that will listen—some true and some just plain bull.

10. Fireplace is southwestern stucco. It makes the family feel like they're gathered around a campfire.

11. Western-style sofa with colorful Indian blanket.

12. Cactus plant that Bubba has spoken many harsh words to and threatened to shave with a chain saw.

13. Boots thrown in corner. Let's hope "someone" didn't forget to wipe off the manure.

14. Wooden, hand-painted buffalo—a lucky find at a garage sale.

15. Handwoven Indian blanket on wall and rug under coffee table. Bought at a western festival last spring.

16. Old spurs, found at a flea market—going up in value every day.

17. Hat on chair. This one lost its shape months ago—no one obeys the "hat rules" all the time.

Western Furniture & Accessories for the Homestead

Follow your heart to the West by decorating your homestead with touches of the frontier. Feel the freedom and independence of the West by not being bound to a "style correctness." Don't worry about following someone's rules. So go ahead, bring the big outdoors in and enjoy your own home on the range with help from mail-order companies. The sky's the limit.

Enjoy pillows and accessories from Western Custom.

Any buckaroo would be thrilled to sleep in this handcrafted canopy bed from R & A Enterprises.

If you're looking for fine furniture that says Southwest, Doolings of Santa Fe will be glad to help you.

Put an authentic Texas longhorn skull from Heads West in your western decorating.

Only the best tanned calfhides are used in Copper Star Cattle & Trading Co. works of art. Furniture is precision handcrafted.

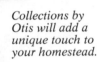

Collections by Otis will add a unique touch to your homestead.

Crystal Farm uses the natural shed antlers for their works of art—mirrors, chandeliers, chairs, and tables.

Decorating by Mail Order

Consider mail order for finding Old West decor. Two magazines, *Country Sampler's WEST* and *Yippy Yi Yea* (see page 125), have tremendous articles and many advertised products to help you on the trail to western decorating.

Collections by Otis
P.O. Box 967
Bristow, OK 74010
(918) 367-9954
Western decorative accessories.
Brochure $3.

Copper Star Cattle & Trading Co.
P.O. Box 10066
Amarillo, TX 79116
(800) 828-0442
Calfhide accessories and southwestern furniture.
Catalog $2.

Crystal Farm Antler Chandeliers
18 Antelope Rd.
Redstone, CO 81623
(303) 963-2350
Line of antler lighting fixtures and furniture. Brochure.

Doolings of Santa Fe
525 Airport Road
Santa Fe, NM 87501
(505) 471-5956

Fine southwestern furniture. Color catalog $5.

Heads West
Box 3037
Ozona, TX 76943
(800) 880-4323
Cattle skulls and other products.
Brochure $2.

M.C. Limited
P.O. Box 17696,
Whitefish Bay, WI 53217
(800) 236-5224
Steerhides, fine leathers, and throw pillows. Free brochure.

R & A Enterprises
5736 Fanwood
Lakewood, CA 90713
(310) 867-4359
Buckaroo beds.
Free brochure.

Western Custom
474 Price Lane
Arlee, MT 59821
(406) 726-4211
Custom crafted accessories.
Brochure $2.

M.C. Limited can help you put the finishing touches on your western decorating with this steerhide.

Cowtown Mailboxes

Country people are highly inventive, spending many hours, even days, designing and building personalized mailboxes. A trip to get the mail is never boring. Here are a few styles to get your creative juices flowin'.

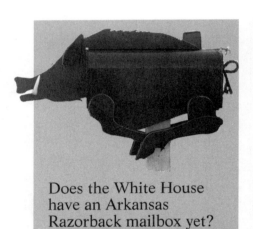

Does the White House have an Arkansas Razorback mailbox yet?

Automatic junk-mail shredder.

Some mail is just full of bull.

Country men never out-grow their love for trains.

John Deere would be impressed.

Even if you don't own a horse, this mailbox makes it look like you do.

If you're looking for the unusual and don't have the time to make it yourself, Curly's Metal Art will fashion a custom mailbox to your liking.
Curly Leiker, Sweetwater Ranch, 2398 Codell Rd., Victoria, KS 67671 (913) 628-8161

Country people know all about "pumping iron," they invented it.

Put the bills in the "udder" mailbox, please.

The Pickup: The Cowboy's Cadillac

Λll cowboys know a pickup is in the direct ancestral line of the horse. Most cowboys have a primal attachment to this mode of transportation. You always know you're in a true cowpoke town by the large number of pickup trucks at the local barbecue pit. Most cowboys take great pride in their trucks. They are known affectionately as the "cowboy's Cadillac." Keeping that pickup in perfect condition as the years take their toll can be hard, if not downright impossible, with all that towin', haulin', and cruisin'. When tradin' time comes around, a cowboy is ready to go out looking for a new "horse."

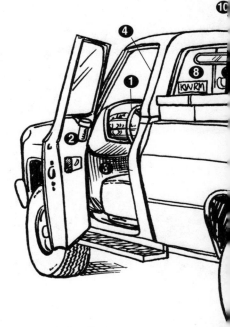

Museums

Chevyland U.S.A.
Exit 257, I-80
Elm Creek, NE 68348
(308) 856-4208
Considered to be the country's most complete Chevy collection and the only museum in the U.S. devoted to the Chevy.

Towe Ford Museum
1106 Main Street
Deer Lodge, MT 59722
(406) 846-3111
The most complete collection of antique Fords, with every year and model represented from 1903 to 1952.

1. Can be driven 200 or more miles with the oil light on.
2. Plastic pop holder, free from Billy Bob's Barbecue.
3. Gimmie cap on seat from J.D.'s Feed and Farm Supply.
4. Tape player blaring out a George Strait hit.
5. American flag . . . and proud of it.
6. Gun rack for hunting season.
7. Bolo tie hanging from mirror.
8. Favorite country music radio station sticker. Keeps waiting for the DJ to announce his number for the all-expenses-paid trip to Opryland.
9. In glove compartment: tapes by Reba McEntire, Garth Brooks,

Alan Jackson, Randy Travis, Brooks and Dunn, and Wynonna Judd; old rodeo tickets; packets of salt, pepper, catsup, mustard, and napkins from McDonald's.

10. On the dashboard: old receipts from feed store, lumber yard, and western clothes

17. Hat caddy mounted on ceiling for favorite western hat.
18. Empty gas can in case this cowboy rides too long on empty.
19. Fishing pole attached to wall of truck bed, in case there's a good fishing hole on the way home from work.
20. Good tires, 'cause everyone depends on this cowboy's truck.

shop; maps; sunglasses, pens that don't write; favorite jerky waiting to be opened.
11. Empty oil bottles. Real men still change their own oil.
12. Toolbox containing tools from Sears, a chain saw, and bailing wire just in case something needs fixin'.
13. Hitch for bass boat and horse trailer.
14. Leftover hay that the wind will eventually blow away.
15. Bumper stickers.
16. Extra tire. Who needs a tow truck?

Did Ya Know?

In 1982, the sales of light trucks—minivans, sports-utility vehicles, and pickup trucks—equaled 25% of auto sales. By 1987, they jumped to 45% of car sales, and by the second quarter of 1992 the rate had climbed to 55% with pickup trucks accounting for 20% of all new vehicle purchases. Keep truckin' America!

Old West Animal Trivia

Buffalo: The American bison will forever stand in western history as the "buffalo" of the plains. When America was discovered, one-third of the continent was covered with these 2,000-pound, five- to six-foot-tall mammals. Buffalo were known for their stupidity and could stampede at a moment's notice. The western expression "plumb buffaloed" means to be confused and too puzzled to know what to do.

The cowboy called eggs "hen fruit."

Dogie: "A calf who has lost his mammy and whose daddy has run off with another cow." This was one way the cowboy described an orphan calf who was in bad shape.

Hereford: A breed of white-faced cattle. Also, a cowman's name for a full-dress suit, because of its white front.

Longhorn: A symbol of the cowboy and the Old West. This fierce and hardy breed of cattle was the first to range in North America and played a major role in the history of Texas and the economic growth of the American West. Without the longhorn, the cowboy as we know him today would not have existed.

Cowboys call the position cows get into when rising from the ground "the prayin' cow."

Country is Chick · PRCA · EZ-LIFE · Cowboys VOTE for Preparation H · I ♥ MY HOSS

A Rear View of Country: Bumper Stickers

If you need to get your message out, do it the American way, with a bumper sticker. Here are a few to enjoy:

Jeans by Wrangler, Body by Doritos

This Truck Stops at Possum Crossings

Warning: Trespassers Will Be Violated

Remember the Alimony

Cowchips Make Great Organic Frisbees

Warning: This Car Makes Sudden Stops for Garage Sales

When the Going Gets Tough Everyone Leaves

I Can't Be Overdrawn, I Still Have Some Checks Left

I've Been Dieting for a Week and All I've Lost Is Seven Days

I'm Mechanically Inclined: I Screw Up Everything

A Fool and His Gold Are Soon Partying

Clogging Is Not a Drain Problem

My Other Car Is a John Deere

Ridin', Ropin', and Rodeo

Catch the Fever—Country Music

Individualists of the World—Unite

Caution: Stunt Driver

Have You Hugged Your Hoss Today?

Country Catalogs

Ever since Ward's and Sears have had mail-order catalogs, country people have had a love affair with this convenient way of shopping. Catalogs made shopping easier for rural Americans and made going to the big city almost unnecessary. In their early history, catalogs were not only "dream books" for many, but the "Charmin" toilet paper of its day—known as "strikin' paper."

Here are several catalogs that will bring some country into your life:

Bass Pro Shops Outdoor World
1935 S. Campbell
Springfield, MO 65807
(800) 227-7776
"The world's greatest sporting goods store." On your way to Branson, stop and see this 150,000 sq. ft. sports paradise.

The Country Loft
2165 N. Forbes Blvd.
Tucson, AZ 85745
(800) 225-5408
Country treasures.

John Deere
1400 Third Ave.
Moline, IL 61265
(800) 544-2122
Home, lawn, and garden supplies.

Mark Allen Productions
3750 S. Valley View, #14
Las Vegas, NV 89103
(800) 858-5568
Roping kits, western replica guns, knives, and tomahawks. Videos and books on the art of the fast draw, plus trick and fancy roping.

Plow & Hearth
301 Madison Rd.
Orange, VA 22960
(800) 627-1712
Country living products.

For the Animals

Ryon's
2601 N. Main
Fort Worth, TX 76106
(800) 725-7966
Saddles and ranch supplies.

Horse Magazines
Horse & Rider
P.O. Box 529
Mount Morris, IL 61051
(800) 435-9610

Western Horseman
P.O. Box 542
Mount Morris, IL 61051
(800) 877-5278
"The World's Leading Horse Magazine Since 1936."

The Meadow Tree Review
(800) 223-6678
A horse lover's dream catalog.

Smith Brothers Roping Supplies
I-35 and Ropers Rd.
Denton, TX 76201
(800) 433-5558
Catalog has one of the largest selections of ropes, bits, and tacks available.
Smith Bros. I-35 Arena: Numerous steer-roping and calf-roping events.
(817) 565-0886

Wholesale Veterinary Supply
(800) 435-6940
Products for pets, livestock, and farm supplies.

Down-Home Museums

The Country Doctor Museum
515 Vance St.
Bailey, NC 27807
(919) 235-4165
Finally, proof that doctors really did make house calls.

Laura Ingalls Wilder-Rose Wilder Lane Home and Museum
Rock Ridge Farm
Mansfield, MO 65704
(417) 924-3626
A must for *Little House on the Prairie* fans. Wilder's famous stories were written here.

Lum 'N Abner Museum
State Highway 88
Pine Ridge, AR 71966
(501) 326-4442
Housed in the museum are photographs and memorabilia tracing the career of Lum 'N Abner's famous radio show, which spanned 25 years.

Chapter
3

THE RIGHT
LINGO

Down-Home Talkin'

Anything that has been said can be said better with down-home talkin'. Country expressions are outrageous and colorful. So lighten up and be as "happy as a dead hog in the sunshine."

A country mile; a far piece A long distance.

Agitated as a June bug In a tizzy.

Ain't fitten to roll with a pig Of no account.

Ain't it the truth! Exclamation.

A poke A sack or bag.

A tall At all.

Bald prairie Bare land.

Banjo belly A man with a pot belly.

Barkin' at a gnat Trying to do the impossible.

Barkin' up the wrong tree Going in the wrong direction.

Bellywasher Beverage.

Bet your boots Guaranteed to happen, a sure thing.

Bidness Business.

Biggety Snobbish.

Big ol' Enormous, huge, immense.

Bless his heart Expression of sympathy and affection.

Booger An affectionate term used to describe someone as a clever little troublemaker.

Boy howdy! This is not a greeting but an exclamation of amazement or surprise.

Buckaroo A term for small children; a friend or pal.

Buffalo chip Cow dropping.

Calm as a dead fish Quiet in disposition.

Cow pattie Cow dropping.

Crooked as a dog's hind leg Sneaky.

Cutter 1. Someone who is a clever devil; a wheeler-dealer. 2. A ranch horse who can single out a calf from a herd.

Dang! Exclamation. "Dang! What a shame!"

Dinner on the ground A picnic.

Don't pay me no never mind Don't pay any attention to me.

Dude A city slicker.

Dumb as an ox Stupid.

Fire-spittin' mad Real mad.

Fixin' to About ready to do something. "He's fixin' to leave."

Foot-stompin' good Very good, good enough to make you want to dance.

Get down and come in A friendly greeting; welcome.

Girl A term used affectionately to address any female, young or old.

Give a holler Call me, keep in touch.

Gussied up All dressed up.

Hanker To want or long for something.

He'll never drown in sweat

He's a lazy person.

Her lips ain't no prayerbook She's a liar.

Her tongue wags at both ends She's a talkative person.

He's a little short between the ears He's slow.

He's not worth dried spit He's an unworthy character.

Hippins Diapers.

Hoedown Party.

Hog heaven A state of total,

Old West Cowboy Lingo

Airtights Canned goods.

All horns and rattles Someone displaying their temper.

Axle grease Butter.

Bachelor A lone ranger.

Bad medicine Bad news.

Baldy A treeless mountaintop.

Beef tea Green, stagnant, shallow water that's full of cow urine.

Bone orchard A cemetery.

Bone-seasoned Experienced.

Canned cow Canned milk.

Can openers or **hooks** Spurs.

Giggle talk Foolish speech.

Hot rock Biscuit.

Iron power A six-shooter.

Jingle your spurs! A command to get a move on, or hurry up.

Live on jawbone Someone living on credit.

Saddle bums Unemployed drifters who would ride from ranch to ranch to get free grub.

Sinbuster A preacher.

Sodbuster A farmer.

Talking iron Another name for the cowboy's six-gun.

Wagon manners Good behavior.

Water-shy Describes any cowboy who didn't like taking a bath.

absolute happiness.

Hoof it To get a move on or move faster.

Hoot and holler 1. When used as a verb it means to carry on, to act up. 2. As a noun it refers to a person who is fun-loving and wild.

Hotter than a two-dollar pistol A compliment. Refers to someone who is going places.

House moss The same as dust bunnies, but more.

Huntin' for a whisper in a big wind Trying to do the impossible.

If she gets to heaven she'll ask to see the upstairs For someone hard to please.

In high cotton Well off and sittin' pretty.

It's nice to have to squint your eyes again The sun has finally come out after a long time of cloudiness.

Kickers 1. Boots. 2. Cowboys or cowgirls who are good dancers.

Laugh and scratch To have a good time or enjoy oneself.

Ma'am After the word "mama," country boys learn this polite word, and use it for the rest of their lives when referring to females. It is also used

for "What?" and "Huh?"

Maverick 1. An unbranded cow. 2. A person who is independent.

Meadow muffin 1. Cow manure dropping. 2. An endearing term for a woman.

More guts than you could hang on a fence A phrase for someone with a lot of courage.

Muled up Mad and stubborn all at the same time.

Mullygrubs Depressed.

Ol' country boy Used for any male acquaintance no matter what age or status.

Over yonder Any place farther away than several feet from where you're standing, such as across town, down the street, or even in another country.

Peesplasher Indoor toilet.

Pistol Someone who is pleasantly ornery.

Rattletrap Jalopy, run-down car.

Right neighborly Friendly, helpful, kind.

Right smack dab A certain location.

Right thar A specific place or location. "The paper you are looking for is right thar."

She's a mess! This is a compliment. A person is witty and entertaining if he or she is a mess.

She's got her trottin' har-

ness on She's able to do anything.

S'posen What if.

Sure don't No.

Tear squeezer A sad story, or anything a cowboy calls sad.

Took a heart burnin' Fell in love.

Well, I swan! An exclamation of wonder.

When she makes pancakes they only got one side to them they're so thin She's a stingy person, a very stingy person.

Won't amount to a hill of beans Unimportant.

Yahoo A rural resident.

Y'all come back, ya hear now? A friendly way of showing hospitality and inviting you back again; your company was enjoyed.

Young'uns The kids.

Colorful Expressions

• You need that like a pig needs a saddle.

• As lazy as the hound that leaned against the fence to bark.

• As quiet as a worm coughing.

• I'm going to cloud up and rain all over you.

• He's as confused as a termite in a yo-yo.

• Busy as a one-armed paper hanger.

• Cold as a gravestone in January.

• So crowded you have to go outside to change your mind.

• Lower than a mole's belly button on diggin' day.

• Slippery as a hog on ice.

• He lies so much he has to get his wife to call the dog for him.

• If his brains were dynamite, he couldn't blow his nose.

• If you put his brains in a bluebird, it'd fly backwards.

• His head is thick as Mississippi mud.

• He's so dumb he'd hold a fish underwater to drown it.

49

- As mad as a rooster in an empty hen house.

- He doesn't know crap from apple butter.

- Sneeze! Your brains are dusty.

- I'm so down I feel like I've been jerked through a knothole backwards.

- So poor the bank won't let him draw breath.

- Flattery is like perfume . . . inhale it, don't swallow it.

- Got about as much chance as a grasshopper in a hen house.

- If frogs had wings they wouldn't bump their butts.

- Grinnin' like a baked possum.

- That really melts my butter.

- Happy as a clam at high tide.

- So ugly she'd make a freight train take a dirt road.

- He's so ugly his daddy had to tie a pork chop around his neck so the dog would play with him.

- You laid this egg and now you want me to hatch it.

- Tomorrow's just the same soup, different bowl.

- So ugly that when he lays on the beach the tide won't come in.

- Nervous as a long-tailed cat in a room full of rocking chairs.

- So poor I can't go window shopping.

- Scarce as hen's teeth.

- He's so thin he has to stand up twice to cast a shadow.

- So nervous she could thread a sewing machine with it runnin'.

- You're so slow that if they hang me, I hope they send you after the rope.

- He's as quick as a herd of turtles.

- She has two speeds: slow and slower.

- Her tongue is loose at both ends.

- It's as true as bacon is pork.

- More money than a porcupine has quills.

- You'd worry the warts off a frog.

- You need that like a tomcat needs a wedding license.

- As happy as a bug in a tater patch.

- Tight as ten toes in a sock.

Chapter
4

THE COWBOY...
AMERICA'S
HERO

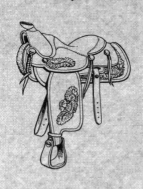

The Singing Cowboys

Roy Rogers and Trigger

America has always been fascinated with the real cowboy. In the process we have made him a true national hero of our culture. In fact, once the cowboy lassoed and corralled our national imagination, he never let it go. To understand the singing cowboy, it is necessary to take a look at the real cowboy.

Surprisingly, the cowboy's reign in its purest form only lasted approximately 25 years, from the close of the Civil War to the late 1800s. Unlike the pulp heroes read about by millions, the true cowboy found few bad guys to fight or maidens to rescue. (What a shame.) Instead of glamour and glitz, he was surrounded by extremes of weather and monotonous work with tortuously long hours in the saddle, only to collect a meager pay at month's end. It was those long hours in the saddle that gave the cowboy the stiff characteristics of his walk, and even when he danced he brought that style with him. (If Preparation H were available then he would have bought it by the gallon.)

The cowboy, in the 1800s, was a hired hand with a job to do. He had no home or mort-

52

gage payments to worry about. His home was the wide open space of the Wild West. With no roads or fences, he rode his horse, driving cattle across the range. There were several abilities he needed to possess: to ride well, control a herd, rope cattle, and endure the primitive living conditions. The cowboy lived a life of freedom, and it's no surprise his lifestyle has been romanticized through the years, especially in our regimented age of big government and computers.

Even though the singing cowboys helped put the "western" in country and western music, and encouraged country singers to wear western clothes, their music had little to do with real cowboys. They were Hollywood's answer to jump start a dying western-movie industry.

Real cowboys did sing songs, but it was to give them some relief from their hard work and help quiet the cattle. It has been said there were only three or four melodies in their western music. Poems and verses were added to these when anyone needed a "new" song.

Around the 1860s, the dime novels made the cowboy the "superman" of his day. He could lasso lightning, ride cyclones, and his rope could round up anything that moved. The dime novels were replaced by the action-packed illustrated covers of the western pulp magazines during the 1920s and 1930s. By the 1940s, mass-market western paperbacks saturated the marketplace.

It was inevitable that the silver screen would romanticize the cowboy and the Wild West just as the dime novels did. William S. Hart, the first "realist" cowboy, became a model for the cinema cowboy and the wild frontier. Hart focused on the ready, but rough and tough, cowboy who alone would confront the elements and stand tall for honesty, courage, and loyalty. Many others followed in his boot prints, including Ken Maynard, who became known as "the World's Champion Cowboy." Maynard was a popular star and did all his own stunts and trick horseback riding. Tom Mix and his bigger-than-life "wonder horse," Tony, caught the imagination of America and Europe during the 1920s. Mix, a silent-screen star, was athletic and in excellent

> "I think the cowboy attitude is really the American attitude from the early days, and it's spreading bigger and better. There's a thread that runs through all of them—to stand up for what you believe in, face things up front and be honest."
>
> Country singer Chris LeDoux, *Country Song Roundup* magazine

became America's way to continue the romance with the Wild West. Gene Autry, Roy Rogers, and Tex Ritter were some of the most successful of this musical genre. All three have been inducted into the Country Music Hall of Fame.

Gene Autry, with his yodeling voice and portrayal of the shy, likable cowboy, set many box-office records. Born in Tioga, Texas, in 1907, Autry worked the graveyard shift at an Oklahoma Telegraph office as a young man. While there, Will Rogers heard him sing and strum his guitar and encouraged Autry to go to New York

Gene Autry

and get a radio job. He did and two years later recorded "That Silver-Haired Daddy of Mine," which sold 30,000 copies the first month and millions of copies over the years. His style of singing was greatly influenced by "the Father of Country Music," Jimmie Rodgers. Autry would become the model for other singing cowboys, paving the way for other newcomers to get "back in the saddle again." His list of

condition and also insisted on doing all his own movie stunts. These stunts involved wild rides, leaping over 30-foot chasms, fights, and dangerous rope swings. With his fancy western apparel, intricately carved boots, and 10-gallon hat, Mix encouraged American kids, through commercial tie-ins, to eat Ralston cereal for breakfast, "the breakfast of champions" of that day.

The singing cowboys

Horse Anatomy

If the only horse you know is Mr. Ed, here's a crash course on parts of the horse you should know. As the great Will Rogers said, "A man that don't love a horse, there is something the matter with him."

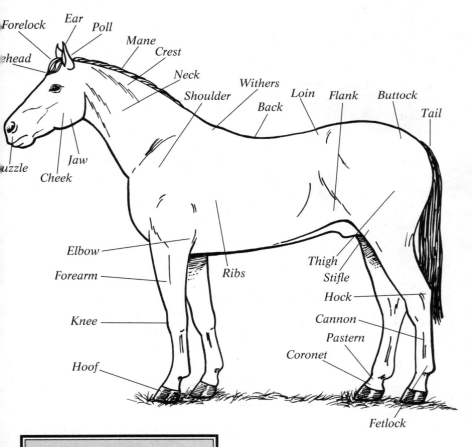

Forelock · Ear · Poll · Mane · Crest · Neck · Shoulder · Withers · Back · Loin · Flank · Buttock · Tail · ehead · Jaw · Cheek · uzzle · Elbow · Forearm · Ribs · Thigh · Stifle · Hock · Knee · Cannon · Pastern · Coronet · Hoof · Fetlock

Did Ya Know?

You can adopt a mustang for $125. If you're thinking "car," then you don't qualify. To find out more, write: U.S. Dept. of the Interior, Bureau of Land Management, Washington, DC 20240.

A Cowboy Saying:

"There's never been a horse that couldn't be rode, there's never been a man that couldn't be throwed."

hit records during the 1930s and 1940s easily made him the most popular singer of his time.

Roy Rogers, born Leonard Slye in Cincinnati, Ohio, in 1912, became a leading motion-picture star, making over 180 movies and TV episodes. In the 1940s, Roy, Dale Evans, and Gabby Hayes, along with their dog, Bullet, and Roy's horse, Trigger, appealed to the masses by fighting outlaws and bringing them to justice. Besides having his own traveling rodeo, TV and radio shows, and recordings, Rogers sang with cowboy musical groups, including the popular Sons of the Pioneers.

Roy was lured from the Sons of the Pioneers into a solo career by Republic Pictures when Gene Autry left over a contract dispute. He was 26 when his first picture, *Under the Western Stars*, was a great hit. Within a few short years, Rogers became America's number-one box-office attraction and one of the nation's most respected and beloved personalities. Together, Roy and Dale became America's ideal sweethearts, and Roy is remembered, to this day, as "The King of the Cowboys."

The western movies, and the singing cowboys from the 1930s through the 1950s, brought an excitement to the cinema that will always be remembered. Along with the cowboys, the fans will never forget the animals who made this period so memorable.

Horses such as Tony, Champion, and Trigger, and a dog called Bullet, were sometimes smarter than their masters, and got them out of many a scrape. Certainly no one will ever forget the singing cowboys, who could shoot a six-shooter more than a dozen times without reloading and who always brought the "varmit" to justice in the nick of time before riding off into the sunset.

Can you match up rider and horse?

Rider	Horse
1. Gene Autry	__ Tony
2. Tonto	__ Tarzan
3. Lone Ranger	__ Buttermilk
4. William S. Hart	__ Diablo
5. Cisco Kid	__ Trigger
6. Roy Rogers	__ Champion
7. Hopalong Cassidy	__ Fritz
	__ Scout
8. Tom Mix	__ Loco
9. Dale Evans	__ Silver
10. Ken Maynard	__ Topper
11. Pancho	

Answers: 1. Champion; 2. Scout; 3. Silver; 4. Fritz; 5. Diablo; 6. Trigger; 7. Topper; 8. Tony; 9. Buttermilk; 10. Tarzan; 11. Loco.

The Western Saddle

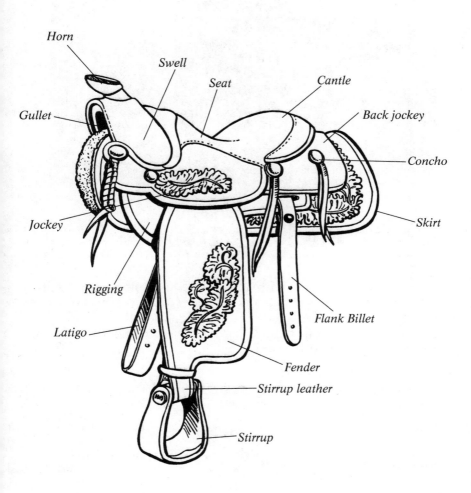

Horn
Swell
Seat
Cantle
Gullet
Back jockey
Concho
Jockey
Skirt
Rigging
Flank Billet
Latigo
Fender
Stirrup leather
Stirrup

An Old West Saying:
"There goes Charlie on his $10 hoss with a $40 saddle."

Did Ya Know?

The cowboy not only sat in the saddle all day and half the night, but used it as a pillow when sleeping.

"Head 'em up, move 'em out," at the East Moreno Ranch!

Horse Packing Trips

Hit the western trail with a pack-trip adventure, a vacation that will make the West come alive for you and your family. Experience the West for yourself, with professional outfitters to guide you, western cowboy food to fill you, and scenery you'll cherish forever.

East Moreno Ranch
P.O. Box 27
Eagle Nest, NM 87718
(800) 282-8778
A six-day "City Slicker Roundup." It's located in the heart of the "Enchanted Circle," a western paradise with riding, roping, trout fishing, campfire meals, and entertainment.

For a list of outfitters, contact:

California Dept. of Fish and Game
3211 S Street
Sacramento, CA 95816
(ask for licensed guides)
(916) 653-7664

Colorado Outfitters Association
P.O. Box 44021
Aurora, CO 80044
(303) 368-4731

Idaho Outfitters and Guides Association
P.O. Box 95
Boise, ID 83701
(208) 342-1919

Montana Outfitters and Guides Assoc.
P.O. Box 9070
Helena, MT 59604
(406) 449-3578

New Mexico Council of Outfitters and Guides
P.O. Box 2008
Albuquerque, NM 87103
(505) 243-4461

Oregon Guides and Packers
P.O. Box 10841
Eugene, OR 97440
(503) 683-9552

Washington Outfitters and Guides Association
P.O. Box 108
Issaquah, WA 98027
(206) 392-6107

Wyoming Outfitters Association
P.O. Box 2284
Cody, WY 82414
(307) 527-7453

Visiting a Dude Ranch

It's a basic right of all Americans to experience being a cowboy or cowgirl at least once in their lifetime. After all, didn't we invent the cowboy? The dude ranch can give every city slicker the chance to play cowboy while on vacation. It's thrilling, safe, and has the romance of the West that every wannabe dreams about. Actually, dude ranches got their start because easterners (you know who you are) couldn't resist the temptation to play cowboy. After visiting and trying on the western ranch lifestyle for size, visitors felt uncomfortable accepting hospitality without compensation. So at the end of the last century, ranches began to charge a small fee—only 10 dollars per week for accommodations, meals, and a good horse to ride. Visitors got the pleasant company of the ranch family to boot.

Though prices have changed a bit, the ranches are still keeping the coffee hot and the fire brightly burning for wannabes.

Preparing to Visit a Dude Ranch

1. Be in good physical condition for high-altitude situations, and some outdoor activities.

2. Be prepared for seeing lots of space, long vistas, many miles with no habitation, and a big sky at night—sometimes it's overwhelming.

3. Prepare for a slower pace of living—activities depend on weather, not time.

4. Take comfortable clothes: worn jeans that are good for riding, long-sleeved shirts, and boots or tie shoes for riding.

5. Bring lotion for the body and lip balm—the West is dry country.

6. Don't forget the camera and plenty of film.

7. A lesson or two on horseback riding is helpful, but dude ranches also have wranglers who would love to teach you how to ride.

See page 72 for more information on dude ranch vacations.

Cowboy Collectibles

For those who woke up to Roy Rogers alarm clocks and carried his lunch pails to school, it may come as a surprise to discover how valuable these cowboy collectibles are today. These memorabilia were commercial tie-ins with popular western radio and TV programs or items sold in department and dime stores from the 1920s through the 1950s. They were mass-produced to satisfy American kids and adults who had fantasies of their own home on the range. Collecting "nostalgia antiques" from the "golden age" of cowboy pop culture is one way to capture

the spirit of the West. With the increasing rage for western decorating and collecting, many of these products are not only escalating in price, but are becoming more difficult to acquire.

Another popular area of collecting is old cowboy gear and things pertaining to our western heritage. The National Bit, Spur and Saddle Collectors Association has members worldwide and is a good source for education and trade shows (see page 72 for address).

Cowboy collectibles are sought after with almost the same fervor as gold during the gold rush days. Even so, many of these "treasures" can still be rounded up at flea markets, antique shops, and from private collectors.

Western memorabilia can be rounded up at Perry's General Store Museum and Antiques, Springfield, Missouri.

For old cowboy gear trade shows, contact the National Bit, Spur and Saddle Collectors Association.

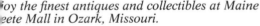

...oy the finest antiques and collectibles at Maine ...ete Mall in Ozark, Missouri.

Hake's Collectibles.

Did Ya Know?

The Lone Ranger, his horse, Silver, and his side-kick, Tonto, rode the air-waves for 22 years.

America's foremost mail- and phone-bid auction house, specializing in character collectibles since 1967. To receive a catalog specializing in pop-culture western memorabilia and other nostalgia collectibles, write:

Hake's Americana & Collectibles
P.O. Box 1444
York, PA 17405
(717) 848-1333

Helpful Books

Collecting the West
by William C. Ketchum, Jr.
A guide to the West and its collect-ibles; over 200 beautiful photos. Ask for it at your local bookstore.

Cowboy Collectibles and Western Memorabilia
by Robert Ball and Ed Vebell Price
A price guide to boots, old western clothes, and gear.
(215) 593-1777

Questions & Answers About the Old West

Q. Which weapon became known as "the gun that won the West"?
A. The 1873 Winchester .44-caliber repeater rifle.

Q. What were some of the nicknames given to an Old West gunfighter?
A. He was often referred to as "bad medicine," a "curly wolf," "leather slapper," a "shootist," and "gun fanner."

Q. Wild Bill Hickok, the frontier scout and marshall, was made into a national hero by what magazine?
A. In 1867, a story appeared in *Harper's Magazine* exaggerating Hickok's exploits. He became a national symbol of the West.

Did Ya Know?

In the Old West all cattle were called "cows," even bulls. A cow is a female of the cattle family two years old or older. A cattle ranch was called a "cow ranch," cattle country was called "cow country," the cowboy's horse was called a "cow horse," and even cowboys who herded only horses were called "cowboys."

Q. "Ace in the hole," during the Old West days, meant what?
A. That a western gunman had a hidden pistol in a secret place for extra protection. Some of those places were in his boot, in his waistband, or in a shoulder holster.

Q. What was famous markswoman Annie Oakley's title in Buffalo Bill's Wild West Show?
A. "Little Sure Shot."

Q. Who was called "cookie," "greasy belly," "belly cheater," and "biscuit shooter" in the Old West?
A. The chuck-wagon cook. He was held in high esteem, and no one dared fool with him or complain about his food. If you did, he'd make sure your taste buds would forever regret it.

Q. The expression "a cowboy sold his saddle" meant what in the Old West?
A. That the cowboy retired from the range.

Q. What world-famous western artist left St. Louis, Missouri, at the age of 16 to become a cowboy?
A. Charles M. Russell, who captured the flavor of the Old West on canvas better than any other artist.

Q. What legendary figure started the first Wild West show and gave the world a glimpse of the Old West?
A. Buffalo Bill, who, at 15, was one of the youngest Pony Express riders and later became the heroic character in over 700 dime novels.

Q. What were several nicknames George Armstrong Custer was known by?
A. As a child, "Curly" and "Cinnamon"; his wife called him "Autie"; Indians knew him as

"Long Hair" and "Son of the Morning Star," but his troops called him "Iron Butt."

Q. How long did the period of time known as the Old West last?
A. Barely 80 years—from the days of Lewis and Clark to the time the great buffalo herds vanished.

Q. What were some of the items, besides food and water, carried in the chuck wagon?
A. Some of the items were: bedrolls, 1/2-inch corral rope, guns, ammunition, lantern, kerosene, axle grease, shovel, ax, branding irons, horseshoeing equipment, extra skillets, and, of course, an extra wagon wheel—the spare tire of the Old West.

Q. Who is credited with the design of the chuck wagon, and how many months' supplies did it carry and for how many men?
A. The cattle baron Charles Goodnight (father of the western cowboys) was given credit for the chuck wagon when in 1866 he rebuilt a surplus army wagon for his trail crew. It carried virtually everything 10 men might need on the prairie for up to five months.

The water barrel could only hold enough water for two days.

Q. What was one of the harsh realities of a cattle drive for the cowboys, and how much was he paid?
A. Trail life was harsh, especially when the chuck wagon ran out of salt and the cowboy was forced to lick horse sweat from his saddle. His pay for three to four months of blisters, thirst, and danger was a mere $100—about enough to buy a fancy pair of boots and a new hat.

Q. What did "five beans in the wheel" mean to Old West gunfighters?
A. To prevent a gun from firing accidentally, many Old West gunmen placed only five bullets ("beans") in their six-shot revolvers, leaving the pistol's hammer resting on an empty cylinder chamber.

Q. What piece of equipment was the Old West cowboy very fussy about?
A. His saddle. The horse was supplied by the employer, but the saddle was the cowboy's own property. It cost him a month's pay or more, but the money was well spent since it lasted for over 30 years.

To get the inside story of the real West, hosted by Kenny Rogers on video, call Columbia House at (800) 638-2922. Some of the titles available are "The Real West," "Buffalo Bill and His Wild West," and more.

Brands of the Old West

In the old days there were no fences and cattle grazed freely, so branding cattle became a necessity. A brand is a mark of ownership (a trademark) placed on cattle, or even horses. Brands were usually burned with a hot iron into the animal's skin. Over the years many different styles emerged, consisting of letters, numbers, symbols, monograms, and many combinations of each—any symbol that represented a certain ranch and was difficult for cattle thieves to alter. Those that did become good at altering brands illegally were called "brand artists." Cowboys were required to be able to read brands and also spot a brand that had been tampered with.

A brand could be placed almost anywhere on the animal and was important to identify ownership, especially since the same brand could be used by another rancher. If the same brand was used by two different cowmen on the same spot of an animal, it would be placed on a different angle. For example, the letter *B* could be slanted, on its side, or straight up.

Rocking heart

Walking 7

R bar four

Lazy T two

Bow and arrow

Bull head

All brands were registered at the county seat or with the cattlemen's association. During big roundups representatives of cattlemen sorted out their own brands (cattle). All cattle brands were checked at loading points. If other cattle were mixed and shipped with a rancher's herd, the inspector credited them to their proper owners by identifying the brand on the cattle.

Branding has been used since antiquity and is a perfect mark of identification. As a cowboy would say, "A brand's something that won't come out in the wash."

Did Ya Know?

Before the invention of barbed wire, pioneers planted thick and thorny osage shrubs that held back cattle, keeping them fenced in. The shrubs were the inspiration for barbed wire. In 1874, Joseph F. Glidden was the first to succeed commercially with his barbed-wire design called "the Winner." By 1890, barbed wire definitely was "the wire that fenced the West," ending the days of the open range and the wandering cowboy. The cowboy called it "bobwire" and

hated and cursed the new fencing.

There were over 800 types of barbed wire invented, and many are highly collectible today. To learn more, read *The Wire That Fenced the West*, a book by Henry and Frances McCallum.

Reading the Best of the West

Ever since Owen Wister blazed the trail with *The Virginian* in 1902, Americans have enjoyed westerns. With the western renaissance we are experiencing today, there's a boom for historical westerns as well as traditional western novels. No matter what your taste in western literature, you'll connect with the past in this time-travel reading adventure.

Dances with Wolves (1988)
by Michael Blake
"He ran the picture of her leaving the arbor over and over in his mind, trying to find something in it to hang on to. But there was a finality about their departure, and it gave him that dreadful feeling of having let something wonderful slip from his hand just as he was picking it up."

The Day the Cowboys Quit
(1971) by Elmer Kelton
"'You ought to find you a woman, Hitch. She'd be good for you, and I know you'd be good for her.' He couldn't tell her he had long wished he had claimed her before Law McGinty did. And he could not tell her he was waiting until he could provide a woman something better than this, for it would seem he was downgrading what Law had given her."

Hondo (1953) by Louis L'Amour
"There was something her father had said, 'We do not own the land, Angie. We hold it in trust for tomorrow. We take our living from it, but we must leave it rich for your son and for his sons and for all of those who shall follow.'"

The Jump-Off Creek (1989)
by Molly Gloss
"But I am used to being Alone, in spirit if not in body, and shall *not* be Lonely, as I never have been inclined that way. I believe what I feel is just a keenness to get to that place and stand under my own roof at last."

Lonesome Dove (1985)
by Larry McMurtry
"He sounded exactly as he always had—hearing his voice so unexpectedly after sixteen years caused her eyes to fill. The sound took the years away."

Riders of the Purple Sage (1912)
by Zane Grey
"Once more her strained gaze sought the sage-slopes. Jane Withersteen loved that wild and purple wilderness. In times of sorrow it had been her strength, in happiness its beauty was her continual delight."

The Virginian (1902)
by Owen Wister
"Lounging there at ease against the wall was a slim young giant, more beautiful than pictures. His broad, soft hat was pushed back; a loose-knotted, dull-scarlet handkerchief sagged from his throat, and one casual thumb was hooked in the cartridge-belt that slanted across his hips. He had plainly come many miles from somewhere across the vast horizon, as the dust upon him showed."

Did Ya Know?

Zane Grey, the western novelist, was a New York dentist. His book *Riders of the Purple Sage,* published in 1912, sold 1.8 million copies. He wrote 50 novels about the West, selling more than 40 million copies.

Louis L'Amour became the "world's bestselling western writer," with almost 225 million books to his credit. *Hondo* was his first major success. John Wayne considered *Hondo* the best western novel he had ever read.

After the Ride.

Western Art

With interest in the West at an all-time high, it's not surprising to see western art booming as well. When someone admires a western scene, it's not only the picturesque beauty that attracts them but the superb storytelling and America's unique western history.

There are many avenues and price ranges to consider when securing your first piece of western art or adding to your present collection. The most expensive are original works of art: oils, acrylics, watercolors, pastels, pencil drawings, mixed media, and sculptures. Less expensive are original prints, photographs, and small sculptures. Next is the limited-edition print market, open editions, and least expensive of all is mass-produced art—found at many department and discount stores. No matter where you shop, it's possible to get good art by a well-known artist or

an up-and-comer, if you know who and what to look for.

For the modest budget, the limited-edition print market is a great source of good western art. Look through magazines that specialize in western art, such as *Southwest Art, Art of the West,* and *U.S. Art* magazine, which carries some western art themes. Then visit art galleries that sell limited-edition prints. These two sources will give

Western Print Available

After the Ride, an acrylic painting (above) by Mike Todd, will be released as a signed open-edition, full-color 14-1/2" x 20" print. The price is $65 (free shipping). Order your print today from:

you a broad overview of the western art genre.

An unframed limited-edition print will usually cost between $125 and $225, though prices can be higher or even lower. Each print is signed and numbered by the artist—this gives the print its value. There's no need to purchase a lower print number, as there is with original prints, because every limited-edition print within an edition is virtually the same.

Besides good art, look for archival, museum-quality, acid-free or ph-neutral, 100 percent rag or buffered paper. These help to keep the print from deteriorating over the years. Also, ask if the inks are colorfast, though all inks fade a little over time.

Contemporary western artists to look for in the limited-edition print market are: Tom Lovell, Donna Egidi, Frank C. McCarthy, Bev Doolittle, Chuck DeHaan (a rodeo rider turned artist), Gary Carter, Mel Gerhold, Nancy Glazier, Chuck Ren, James Bama, Paul Calle, and Dan Mieduch, among others.

Other sources of great art are museum shows and western art exhibits, where often you will see originals that later will be made into prints. Museums usually focus on old artists of the West, such as Frederic Remington, Charles Russell, George Catlin, and others. Some of the better-known national organizations to contact for art exhibits are: the Cowboy Artists of America (CAA), the Artists of America (AOA), the National Academy of Western Art (NAWA), and the Northwest Rendezvous Group (NWR).

Most of all, buy the print (or original) that satisfies you and brings the West to life.

Glossary of Art Terms

Artist's Remarque: A small hand-painted or drawn picture on a limited-edition print done by the artist and usually placed in the border.

Certificate of Authenticity: Most publishers offer a guarantee of the authenticity of the artist's work and his or her signature on the print, and that the photographic plates were destroyed after the edition's printing.

Edition, Edition Run, Edition Size: The total number of copies printed within a limited edition and written on the print as the bottom half of a fraction, as in 45/1,000. The number 45 is the 45th print in an edition of 1,000. Artist's or publisher's proofs are not included.

Limited-Edition Print: To copy a work of art done originally in another medium by a photomechanical, lithographic offset process (printing) and make a restricted number of identical prints (such as 1,000 prints). Later, all prints are sequentially numbered and signed by the artist.

Open Edition: An unrestricted number of identical prints signed by the artist.

Secondary Market: The resale market for any work of art.

Did Ya Know?

Each year, twenty-five million people buy limited-edition prints. Some prints have been known to rise in value to thousands of dollars. However, most people buy prints because they enjoy the art, not because of the possibility for increase.

The Rodeo

Clint Johnson, 1980, 1987–1988 World Saddle Bronc Riding Champion.

Though there are probably scads of western towns that will take credit for its origin, no one can say when or where the rodeo started. It probably had its beginning out in the middle of dry dirt and sagebrush—the middle of nowhere. Maybe it began with a young cocky cowboy bustin' an outlaw bronc someone claimed no one could ride. Certainly, the everyday duties of the cowpoke, and a little friendly competition among ranch hands, had something to do with it as well. One thing is certain, the rodeo is the roughest and wildest sport in America.

Some rodeos even begin with a grand entry that could best be described as a horse-and-people traffic jam. Except this traffic jam is enjoyed by all. It's a chance to watch an equine parade with the riders dressed in fancy, colorful duds. As everyone trots past the flag, hats are removed and placed over hearts as a gesture of undying love.

The rodeo cowboy is more than an athlete, he lives his sport, many times driving all night to compete the next morning. He lays it all on the line in these life-threatening events.

Rough Stock Events

Saddle bronc riding (rodeo's "classic event"), bareback riding, and bull riding are all timed events. In the Old West, ranch hands competed with each other to see who could ride a wild horse with the most style. The rodeo cowboy of today has eight seconds to show his stuff. In bronc-riding events (with or without a saddle), the rider is required to press his dulled spurs into the horse's side and

68

shoulders. In bull riding it's not required, but if the cowboy proves insane enough to do so, he'll garner extra points and maybe some extra bruises as well!

Timed Events

Timed events are a race against the clock and the other contestants. These, no doubt, were born out of ranch work and include calf roping, steer roping and wrestling, and team roping. Calf and steer roping are similar.

The calf or steer is given a prescribed head start, the cowboy gives chase on horseback, ropes the animal's neck (horns in steer roping), the horse stops, and the cowboy dismounts and securely ties any three legs of the animal. The cowboy quickly raises his hands to signal his run is finished. He remounts his horse, slackens the rope, and the calf or steer must remain tied for six seconds.

Steer wrestling pits a cowboy against a 450- to 750-pound steer. On horseback, the cowboy pursues the steer, who has a head start. Once he's alongside he leaps off his horse, taking the steer by the horns and twisting its head until the steer falls to the ground. And it all takes place in a few seconds.

Team roping involves two horsemen. One cowboy ropes the steer's head or horns while

the other ropes its hind legs. Both ropers' horses must face the steer with ropes taut and wrapped counterclockwise around their saddle horns when finished.

There is one timed event strictly for the cowgirls—barrel racing. This event ranks right after bull riding in crowd popularity. A rider races her equine athlete in a cloverleaf pattern around three barrels, hopefully without knocking any down. Whoever has the fastest time wins. The competition is so close among these top cowgirls that electronic timers accurate to within a hundredth of a second must be used.

No rodeo is complete without those crazy-as-a coot, off-the-wall clowns. Yet, they serve as more than entertainers. They are there to divert an angry bronc or crazed bull from trampling or falling on a cowboy, or to rescue a rider whose hand is caught in the rigging— they save lives.

The rodeo also provides specialty acts of slapstick comedy, trick ropers, trick riders, animal acts, and clown acts. These entertainers help to keep the little buckaroos not only entertained, but from begging for more hot dogs and popcorn.

Did Ya Know?

In her nine years of pro competition, nine-time barrel racing world champion Charmayne Rodman, riding her legendary horse, Scamper, has collected over $1 million, making Charmayne the first and only "million-dollar cowgirl."

All-Time PRCA Career Earnings Leaders

(Through 1992)

Roy Cooper
(CR, SR, TR, SW)*.......$1,374,953
Dee Pickett
(CR, TR).......................$1,191,262
Lewis Feild
(SB, BB, TR)................$1,163,340
Tom Ferguson
(CR, SW, TR, SR)........$1,145,880
Chris Lybbert
(CR, SW, TR)...............$1,073,158
Bruce Ford
(BB)...........................$1,064,570
John W. Jones, Jr.
(CR, SW, TR).................$983,846
Tuff Hedeman
(BR, SB, TR)..................$963,325
Clay O'Brien Cooper
(TR, CR, SW).................$961,554
Mike Beers
(TR, CR, SR)..................$944,448
Tee Woolman
(TR, SR, CR)..................$915,160
Ty Murray
(SB, BB, BR)..................$897,811
Ted Nuce
(BR)..............................$888,714

*SB: saddle bronc riding; BB: bareback riding; BR: bull riding; CR: calf roping; SW: steer wrestling; TR: team roping; SR: steer roping

Did Ya Know?

Country singers not only entertain at rodeos, but some, at one time, have even been contestants: Reba McEntire, Chris LeDoux, and Moe Bandy, to name a few. Even some famous spouses, such as Sandy Brooks, Garth's wife, have been rodeo participants.

Highest Annual Earnings:
$258,750 by 22-year-old Ty Murray in 1991.

Most Money Won at a Rodeo:
$101,531 by Billy Etbauer at the 1992 National Finals Rodeo.

Top 10 Rodeos of 1992

1. **National Finals Rodeo**
   Las Vegas, NV $2,590,770
2. **Houston Livestock Show and Rodeo**
   Houston, TX $400,052
3. **Cheyenne Frontier Days Rodeo**
   Cheyenne, WY $357,251
4. **National Western Stock Show**
   Denver, CO $355,078
5. **San Antonio Livestock Exposition Rodeo**
   San Antonio, TX $318,766
6. **Reno Rodeo**
   Reno, NV $306,198
7. **Southwestern Exposition Livestock Show and Rodeo**
   Fort Worth, TX $284,234
8. **Dodge National Circuit Finals Rodeo**
   Pocatello, ID $262,000
9. **California Rodeo**
   Salinas, CA $198,262
10. **Pendleton Round-up Rodeo**
    Pendleton, OR $192,707

Rodeo Associations

Canadian Professional Rodeo Association (CPRA)
223 2116 27th Ave. N.E.
Calgary, Alberta, Canada T2E7A6
(403) 250-7440

Professional Rodeo Cowboys Association (PRCA)
101 Pro Rodeo Dr.
Colorado Springs, CO 80919
(719) 593-8840

Women's Professional Rodeo Association (WPRA)
Route 5, Box 698
Blanchard, OK 73010
(405) 485-2277

Rodeo Cowboy After OSHA*

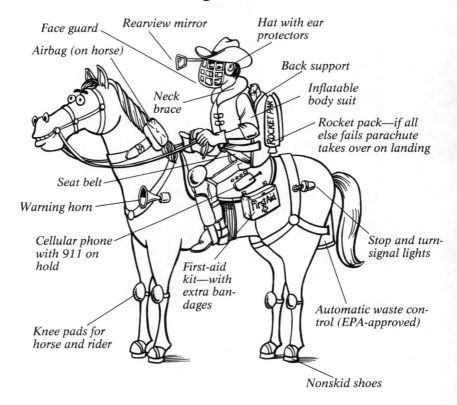

Face guard

Rearview mirror

Hat with ear protectors

Airbag (on horse)

Back support

Neck brace

Inflatable body suit

Rocket pack—if all else fails parachute takes over on landing

Seat belt

Warning horn

Cellular phone with 911 on hold

First-aid kit—with extra bandages

Stop and turn-signal lights

Automatic waste control (EPA-approved)

Knee pads for horse and rider

Nonskid shoes

*OSHA: Occupational Safety and Health Administration.
(OSHA doesn't know a cowboy is a man with a horse, guts, and brains.)

71

Dude Ranch Vacations

The Dude Ranchers' Association
P.O. Box 471, Laporte, CO 80535
(303) 223-8440
These folks are friendly and helpful.

Send $3 for a directory of over 100 dude ranches.

Old West Dude Ranch Vacations
(800) 444-DUDE
"The Civilized Way to Rough It." They will help you package a dude ranch vacation free of charge. Free catalog.

Ranch Vacations
by Gene Kilgore
(800) 222-4229, ex. 74
A terrific guide for $18.95.

Western Museums

Amon Carter Museum
3501Camp Bowie
Fort Worth, TX 76107
(817) 738-1933

Barbed Wire Museum
220 West First
La Crosse, KS 67548
(913) 222-9900

Buffalo Bill Historical Center
720 Sheridan Avenue
Cody, WY 82414
(307) 587-4771

Charles M. Russell Museum
400 13th St. North
Great Falls, MT 59501
(406) 727-8787

The Cowboy Artists of America Museum
1550 Bandera Highway
Kerrville, TX 78028
(512) 896-2553

Eiteljorg Museum
500 W. Washington St.
Indianapolis, IN 46204
(317) 636-9378

Frederic Remington Art Museum
303 Washington St.
Ogdensburg, NY 13669
(315) 393-2425

Gene Autry Western Heritage Museum
4700 Western Heritage Way
Los Angeles, CA 90027
(213) 667-2000

Gilcrease Museum
1400 Gilcrease Museum Rd.
Tulsa, OK 74127
(918) 596-2700

National Cowboy Hall of Fame
1700 N.E. 63rd St.
Oklahoma City, OK 73111
(405) 478-2250

National Cowgirl Hall of Fame Western Heritage Center
515 Avenue B, Hereford, TX 79045
(808) 364-5252

Pro Rodeo Hall of Fame and Museum of the American Cowboy
101 Pro Rodeo Dr.
Colorado Springs, CO 80919
(719) 593-8840

Roy Rogers and Dale Evans Museum
15650 Seneca Rd.
Victorville, CA 92392
(619) 243-4547

Tom Mix Museum
721 N. Delaware, Dewey, OK 74029
(918) 534-1555

Bits, Spurs & Saddles

Cowboy Spurs and Their Makers
by Jane Pattie
Texas A&M University Press, Drawer C, College Station, TX 77845
A must for cowboy fans and collectors, $39.95.

National Bit • Spur & Saddle Collectors Association
P.O. Box 3098
Colorado Springs, CO 80934
(719) 473-7101
Helping to preserve the heritage of western Americana. Newsletter and membership $20 annually.

Chapter
5

IT'S IN THE
MUSIC

The Music Is Called Country

Alan Jackson

Country music can be many things to many people, for it is a term that describes several styles of music all wrapped up under one all-inclusive heading. Originally it was music played in the countryside by farmers and ranchers and common working people, creating "down-home" entertainment for themselves, their families, and their friends. The music was based on folk music and dancing tunes that immigrants brought with them from England, Ireland, and Scotland, while other musical influences came from Europe and Africa. All of these musical forms melded together in the southern part of the United States and spread to the Southwest, becoming what we know today as "country music."

Over the years country music has embraced many musical styles, such as old-time music, blues, western, Cajun, bluegrass, western swing, gospel music, honky tonk, the "Nashville Sound," and rockabilly or country rock. Today, country music is a blend of the best of what has come before. No other form of popular music has endured such change. Yet country music has not only survived—it's in the driver's seat of American music for the first time in its history.

It all started 70 years ago, or thereabouts. (Some historians are still debating when the earliest country music recordings were made.) Fiddlers A. C. "Eck" Robertson and Henry Gilliland decided to take a train from Virginia to New York to see about this new business of making phonograph records. Unannounced, but with good ol' boy friendliness, they showed up at Victor Records—Robertson was dressed as a cowboy and Gilliland as a Confederate soldier. The Victor people were so amused they took them in and recorded several songs, including Robertson's fiddle tune "Sallie Gooden," one of the most famous songs in country music history.

At the time, this style of mountain tunes and folk blues of southern rural whites was not called country music. The music got its first name when Ralph Peer, an Okeh Records executive, labeled a string band he had recorded the Hill Billies. Later the music became known as "hillbilly music." Country's first million-selling record was "The Prisoner's Song," recorded by Vernon Dalhart in 1924. Dalhart was, surprisingly, a Broadway performer who saw a career opportunity in the rural record market. But most early commercial country music performers were common laborers—farmers, mill workers, railroad men, carpenters, coal miners, and cowboys.

The radio barn-dance pro-grams of the early 1920s fueled the growth of this new music. WSM's National Barn Dance in Nashville later became a three-hour program known as the Grand Ole Opry. Country music began reaching millions of homes when the NBC radio network started broadcasting a portion of the Grand Ole Opry each Saturday night. (This program is still running, making it America's longest running radio show.) In the 1930s, Roy Acuff became the Opry's first superstar, and he will always be remembered as "the King of Country Music."

Within two days of each other, Ralph Peer recorded two of country music's most notable acts—the Carter

Reba McEntire

Wynonna Judd

Family and Jimmie Rodgers. Rodgers got the train rolling and became country music's first superstar. He is referred to today as "the Father of Country Music." Rodgers's music blended black and white elements, which he drew from his experience working as a railroad brakeman. His professional career lasted only six years before tuberculosis ended his life. The Carter Family sang of home, family, and God and were popular entertainers until the early 1940s.

By the late 1930s, movies were depicting the singing cowboy for an adoring America, and this "hillbilly" music, which originated out of the South, was beginning to be called by a more respectable name, "country and western" music.

More than 300,000 juke-boxes were blaring out a hard-edged, up-tempo style of country music by the early 1940s. The electric guitar, piano, string bass, and steel guitar, along with the fiddle, became country music's primary instruments. The nightlife provided new topics for songwriters. Songs about farm life, family, and God were sung less frequently as songwriters explored the new topics of love, heartbreak, loneliness, cheating, and the dangers of drinking and rambling. This musical style, honky tonk, has served as country's backbone for more than half a century. The '40s produced two styles of country music, honky tonk and western swing.

In the early 1960s, traditional country music was faltering under the tidal wave of rock 'n' roll. So, country music

George Strait

sought out nontraditional audiences in Las Vegas, with Patsy Cline being the first country star to appear there. Bob Dylan added his own uniqueness to the music and helped create country rock in the late '60s. Dylan helped take the twang out of country and flung the door wide open for new country artists. The country rock sound, created by a new breed, was a fresh and approachable style that used rock 'n' roll themes and theatrics to reach an even larger audience. Three TV shows, "Glen Campbell's Goodtime Hour," "The Johnny Cash Show," and "Hee Haw," brought country to the masses via the small screen in the late '60s and early '70s. The "crossover" sound of country pop brought Glen Campbell and Kenny Rogers to the forefront during this period.

Garth Brooks

Country music would experience profound changes in the next two decades. The "outlaw" movement began in 1973 when Waylon Jennings recorded his *Honky Tonk Heroes* album. Jennings and Willie Nelson were the most famous of the "outlaws," who were not rebelling against the music itself but against their lack of control over the way the music was recorded.

Two 1980 movies, *Urban Cowboy* and *Coal Miner's Daughter,* encouraged Nashville to make a temporary course change and produce more accessible records with string sections and a pop rhythm. Country-pop artists such as Kenny Rogers, Olivia Newton-John, Crystal Gayle, and others thrived during this time.

Leading the way in the 1980s and 1990s with a back-to-basics sound were the "neo-traditionalists," who drew heavily from older, traditional

Trisha Yearwood

country music: acts like George Strait, Ricky Skaggs, Reba McEntire, Randy Travis, Clint Black, Garth Brooks, Vince Gill, Alan Jackson, Kathy Mattea, and Trisha Yearwood, among others.

These new country artists proved to have the sound America was waiting for. With the advent of the new crop of country performers, country music has grown more than any other form of popular music. In 1990, the CMA Awards ceremony was the top-rated show in its time slot. In 1992, the two-hour CMA Awards show was the third-highest rated program of the week, with a viewership of 48 million. With the popularity of country music growing, this show will no doubt continue to set new records in the years to come.

Garth Brooks, the major force since 1989, catapulted country music into America's consciousness like no other. He alone sold nearly 28 million albums by the end of 1992—no other singer came close. Garth Brooks is the only country artist to release an album (*Ropin' the Wind,* 1991) that in its first week on *Billboard's* pop charts garnered the number-one spot. Between 1989 and 1991, total sales nearly tripled for country music, from approximately $500 million to $1.5 billion.

Once much of America scorned country as the folk music of backward hillbillies, but no more. Today's country music is filled with emotion and memory. That is its heartbeat. Baby boomers and the young alike are catching the country fever, because country music is America's music.

Vince Gill

CMA's Song of the Year 1982–1993

Country music honors its most gifted songwriters as no other form of music does, and for good reason—they have some of the best in the industry. The CMA Song of the Year Award is voted on by more than 6,000 members of the Nashville-based trade organization. Here are the winners for the past 12 years:

1982 "Always on My Mind" by Johnny Christopher, Wayne Carson, and Mark James

1983 "Always on My Mind" by Johnny Christopher, Wayne Carson, and Mark James

1984 "Wind Beneath My Wings" by Larry Henley and Jeff Silbar

1985 "God Bless the USA" by Lee Greenwood

1986 "On the Other Hand" by Paul Overstreet and Don Schlitz

1987 "Forever and Ever, Amen" by Paul Overstreet and Don Schlitz

1988 "80s Ladies" by K. T. Oslin

1989 "Chiseled in Stone" by Max D. Barnes and Vern Gosdin

1990 "Where've You Been" by Jon Vezner and Don Henry

1991 "When I Call Your Name" by Vince Gill and Tim DuBois

1992 "Look at Us" by Vince Gill and Max D. Barnes

1993 "I Still Believe in You" by Vince Gill and John Barlow Jarvis

Match 'Em Up

 est your country music song savvy. How many songs can you match with the correct artist? Write the correct song number next to the artist who sang it.

The Song

1. "On the Other Hand"
2. "All My Exs Live in Texas"
3. "She's in Love with the Boy"
4. "He Stopped Loving Her Today"
5. "When I Call Your Name"
6. "Crazy"
7. "Waiting for a Train"
8. "Where've You Been"
9. "Here in the Real World"
10. "Put Some Drive in Your Country"
11. "I Will Always Love You"
12. "Wichita Lineman"
13. "I Know How He Feels"
14. "Put Yourself in My Shoes"
15. "You're the One"
16. "Living Proof"
17. "What's She Doing Now"
18. "Love Can Build a Bridge"
19. "My Heroes Have Always Been Cowboys"
20. "Before I'm Over You"
21. "She Is His Only Need"
22. "Neon Moon"
23. "Mama Don't Forget to Pray for Me"
24 "Bubba Shot the Jukebox"
25. "Should've Been a Cowboy"
26. "A Cowboy's Been Born with a Broken Heart"

The Artist

___ Wynonna Judd
___ Dwight Yoakam
___ Reba McEntire
___ Randy Travis
___ Clint Black
___ Garth Brooks
___ Loretta Lynn
___ Trisha Yearwood
___ George Jones
___ Alan Jackson
___ Brooks & Dunn
___ Patsy Cline
___ George Strait
___ Jimmie Rodgers
___ Glen Campbell
___ Mark Chesnutt
___ Vince Gill
___ Travis Tritt
___ Diamond Rio
___ Dolly Parton
___ Toby Keith
___ Ricky Van Shelton
___ Willie Nelson
___ Boy Howdy
___ Kathy Mattea
___ The Judds

Answers: 1. Randy Travis; 2. George Strait; 3. Trisha Yearwood; 4. George Jones; 5. Vince Gill; 6. Patsy Cline; 7. Jimmie Rodgers; 8. Kathy Mattea; 9. Alan Jackson; 10. Travis Tritt; 11. Dolly Parton; 12. Glen Campbell; 13. Reba McEntire; 14. Clint Black; 15. Dwight Yoakam; 16. Ricky Van Shelton; 17. Garth Brooks; 18. The Judds; 19. Willie Nelson; 20. Loretta Lynn; 21. Wynonna Judd; 22. Brooks & Dunn; 23. Diamond Rio; 24. Mark Chesnutt; 25. Toby Keith; 26. Boy Howdy.

Are You a Closet Country Music Fan?

Country music is taking the music world by the horns. It's the most listened-to format of music on radio today. Yet, there are still "some people" who resist confessin' how much they listen to and love country music. Could you be one of those people? This test will help you decide if you're a true country music fan or just a closet fan.

1. Do you listen to country music when friends aren't around?
___Yes ___No

2. Have you preprogrammed your radio so that you can get to your country stations faster, but hope no one else pushes those buttons?
___Yes ___No

3. When out with friends of "other musical persuasions," do you make excuses to get home early on Saturday night so that you won't miss "The Grand Ole Opry" show?
___Yes ___No

4. Do you tell your friends that you love having cable TV because of the many choices of viewing you have, when in fact the only two stations you watch are CMT and TNN?
___Yes ___No

5. Have you told your friends that you're joining an aerobic-exercise class called "Boot-Scootin' Kickers," when in reality it's a country western dance class?
___Yes ___No

6. When no one's around, do you practice walking in cowboy boots and hat?
___Yes ___No

7. Have your friends ever accused you of trying to talk with a twang?
___Yes ___No

8. Do you tell friends, weeks in advance, that you are "busy" the night of the CMA Awards show, so you can watch it without being interrupted?
___Yes ___No

9. When stopped at a red light, have you ever rolled up your car windows so that no one would hear you listening to country music?
___Yes ___No

Scoring: Let's face it, if you checked only one "yes," you're a closet country music fan.
Remedy: Join the stampede— "it's cool to be country."

Former Jobs of Country Stars

Ricky Van Shelton

Most country singers didn't give up their jobs until the time was right. To be a full-time country entertainer takes perseverance and a lot of hard work. Here's a list of some of the jobs that some stars had before their big break.

Gene Autry	Telegraph operator
Clint Black	Construction worker
Garth Brooks	Pizza maker, jackhammer operator
Billy Dean	Actor in TV commercials
Merle Haggard	Dishwasher
Emmylou Harris	Waitress
Alan Jackson	Driving a forklift at K-Mart
Waylon Jennings	Disc jockey
George Jones	House painter
Hal Ketchum	Master carpenter
Kathy Mattea	Country Music Hall of Fame tour guide
Dolly Parton	Waitress at Shoney's
Mike Reid	NFL lineman with the Cincinnati Bengals
Jimmie Rodgers	Railroad brakeman
Roy Rogers	Fruit picker

Doug Stone	Diesel mechanic
George Strait	Designing cattle pens
Randy Travis	Grilled hamburgers at the Nashville Palace
Travis Tritt	Heating and air-conditioning man
Ricky Van Shelton	Cleaned chicken houses
Hank Williams	Shoe-shine boy, peanut salesman
Tammy Wynette	Beautician
Trisha Yearwood	Receptionist at MTM Records

Music Row Lingo

Located in Nashville, Music Row is the hub for country music's recording and publishing industry. It's considered to have the highest concentration of musical talent on the planet. Here's some lingo used in the industry.

Ax Guitar.
Bullet A small dot or star on the charts that indicates that a song or an album is having strong airplay or sales.
Cut A song on a record or album.
Flacks Public relations people.
Germ Someone who is a very pushy promoter of a song, record, or book.
Hair act Any young male country artist with long hair.
Hat act Any young male country artist who wears a cowboy hat.
Pitch An attempt to get someone in the music business to record your song.
Plugger A person who pitches a song.
Schmooze To work the crowds at a party or any music-industry function just to be noticed.
Shopping Trying to cut a deal for a new artist by bringing his or her work to a record company.
Single A cut (song) from an album that makes the airwaves.
Skins Drums.
The trades Music-industry publications covering what's new, what's hot, and what's not.
Work tape A very simple recording of a song using guitar/vocal or piano/vocal to pitch a song to a publisher.

Books for the Country Songwriter

The Craft & Business of Songwriting
by John Braheny

Everything You Always Wanted to Know About Songwriting
by Cliffie Stone

How to Pitch & Promote Your Songs
by Fred Kolle

The Official Country Music Directory (1993 edition) (619) 322-3858
A reference guide used by music executives and those serious about the country music industry. $80.

The Songwriter's & Musician's Guide to Nashville
by Sherry Bond

Name That Country Song

1. What song took only 20 minutes for Johnny Cash to write, was released in 1956, and became his first pop hit and a million-selling country smash?

2. Name the song that Merle Haggard cowrote with his wife and that went on to be recorded by over 100 artists, including Emmylou Harris, Kenny Rogers, and Loretta Lynn?

3. Written by Hank Williams and released in 1951, it was one of Hank's favorite tunes and garnered his first major accep-tance in pop music. Can you name the song?

4. What song became Jim Reeves's only million-selling single? The inspiration for the song started with a telephone conversation.

5. What was the song Don Gibson wrote in 1958 as repossession men cleaned out his trailer? Ray Charles recorded it in 1962, and Conway Twitty also made it a hit 10 years later.

6. Initially Tammy Wynette disliked this song and even the way she sang it, but it became her signature song, selling five million copies. What is the song?

7. Name the song that in 1952 became the first number-one single by a female country singer and launched the career of Kitty Wells?

8. If Vince Gill and Tim DuBois didn't have their golf game rained out, music history (and Vince) would have certainly missed out on this number-one song. Can you name it?

9. Name the song that was written in a laundry room by Tony Arata. "Somewhere in the spin cycle, the idea all came together," he says. It was one of the singles released from

Garth Brooks's debut album.

10. What song was first named "Don't Break My Heart" and sold over eight million copies after the artist suggested a new title?

11. Clint Black released this song in 1989 and millions of people identified with him. It became the first debut single by a male country artist to reach number one. What was the song?

12. This song is about an ex-girlfriend, but George Jones thought it contained too many "just becauses." In 1962 it was number one for six weeks, and today it is one of his most requested songs. Can you name it?

13. What was the song that was written in one sitting, was inspired by the movie *Dr. Zhivago,* and became the theme song for "Glen Campbell's Goodtime Hour"?

14. What song was Hank Williams's ninth million-seller and subsequently went on to be recorded by more than 100 artists?

15. What song, written by Pee Wee King and Redd Stewart, became Tennessee's official song in 1965?

16. What song did Clint Black write about a guy who dies

in the first line of the song?

17. What was the song that became a number-one hit for George Strait but in the beginning was thought to be too traditionally country to get radio time?

18. What song provided Doug Stone (real name, Doug Brooks) with the idea for his stage name? (Garth Brooks had just released his debut album when Epic records signed Doug to a recording contract, so the executives advised Doug to change his name.)

19. Hal Ketchum grew up in a small town, and his first number-one hit was about a small town. Can you name the song?

20. What song by Trisha Yearwood was the first debut single by a female in 26 years to become a number-one hit on the country music chart?

> ## Did Ya Know?
> • A gold record is one that sells 500,000 copies.
> • A platinum record is one that sells one million copies.

Answers: 1. "I Walk the Line"; 2. "To-day I Started Loving You Again"; 3. "Cold, Cold Heart"; 4. "He'll Have to Go"; 5. "I Can't Stop Loving You"; 6. "Stand by Your Man"; 7. "It Wasn't God Who Made Honky Tonk Angels"; 8. "When I Call Your Name"; 9. "The Dance"; 10. "Achy Breaky Heart"; 11. "A Better Man"; 12. "She Thinks I Still Care"; 13. "Gentle on My Mind"; 14. "Your Cheatin' Heart"; 15. "Tennessee Waltz"; 16. "Wake Up Yesterday"; 17. "Unwound"; 18. "Heart of Stone"; 19. "Small Town Saturday Night"; 20. "She's in Love with the Boy."

Breaking into the Country Music Scene

Organizations

ASCAP
2 Music Square West
Nashville, TN 37203
(615) 742-5000

BMI
10 Music Square East
Nashville, TN 37203
(615) 244-0044

Country Music Association, Inc.
1 Music Circle S.
Nashville, TN 37203
(615) 244-2840

Sesac, In.
55 Music Circle East
Nashville, TN 37203
(615) 320-0055

Songwriters' Association International
1 Music Square West
Nashville, TN 37203
(615) 256-3354

Pickin' & Grinnin' Places

Auditions USA
2802 Opryland Drive
Nashville, TN 37114
(800) 94-STAGE
If you have talent for performing, this could be a break for you. A yearly, national talent search for Opryland USA and Fiesta Texas musical theme parks.

The Bluebird Cafe
4104 Hillsboro Road
Nashville, TN 37215
(615) 383-1461
"Writers night" on Monday. Shows run from

6:00 P.M. to 9:00 P.M.

Country Showdown
63 Music Square East
Nashville, TN 37203
Find out about the regional music contest in

your area (or call your local country radio station). The finalists compete at the Grand Palace in Branson, Missouri. The 1993 winner received a new GMC truck, $50,000, and a recording contract to boot.

Rising Star Talent Productions
P.O. Box 30925
Gahanna, OH 43230
(614) 478-4333
The finalists go to Pigeon Forge for more competition. Many are hired to perform at Dollywood and the Dixie Stampede.

Music Festivals

Grant's Bluegrass and Old Time Music Festival
Route 2, Box 74
Hugo, OK 74743
(405) 326-5598
Over 70 hours of country music and bluegrass from the best. August.

Hank Williams, Sr., Day
127 Rose Street
Georgiana, AL
(205) 376-2396
Enjoy country music and visit the new museum (open all year), which is housed in Hank's childhood home. June.

Jimmie Rodgers Memorial Festival
P.O. Drawer 2170
Meridian, MS 39302
Celebrates the memory of "the Father of Country Music." May.
(601) 483-5763

Musikfest
556 Main St.
Bethlehem, PA 18108
(215) 861-0678
Over 600 acts performing—country, blues, folk, bluegrass and more—in this nine-day music extravaganza. August.

Old Time Fiddlers' Jamboree and Crafts Festival
Smithville Chamber of Commerce
P.O. Box 64
Smithville, TN 37166
(615) 597-4163
One of the biggest and best festivals. July.

The Rocky Gap Country and Bluegrass Festival
320 Greene Street
Cumberland, MD 21502
(301) 724-2511
Country and bluegrass music and crafts. August.

Traditional Music Festival
40404 Berea College
Box 2336
Berea, KY 40403
(606) 986-9341
Ext. 5140
A full weekend of Appalachian music and square dancing. October.

W4 Country Music Weekend
WWWW-FM
Detroit, MI 48231
(313) 259-4323
Fans gather at the Hart Plaza on Mother's Day weekend for three days of country music. May.

Chapter 6

THE MUSIC MAKES THEM SING

---◆---

Country Stars Sing Poetry

Country music has been called the poetry of the common man, for only in country music are the lyrics "king." "We treat the lyrics," said Garth Brooks to *Forbes* magazine, "like the woman any man wants to impress most. We give the lyrics all the attention we can." The lyrics are the key to country music. A country song is a special form of communication, more like two people conversing, more so than any other type of mass-appeal music. When the audience recognizes and approves the sincerity of the performer, a "sincerity contract" is made, creating a special bond between the singer, song, and audience.

Country music is filled with passion, sentiment, and memory. It's about the real world people experience each day, and its themes are many. When the song is about a great relationship between a man and woman, it's called "happy love." When love is having the blues it's called "hurtin' love." Most country songs are in the latter category. "Cheatin" songs can also be found, as well as songs about "livin"—all the hopes, dreams, and experiences of an individual. These are the four broad categories of country music. Songs about God, home, and country have always been an important part of the country music landscape too.

Whatever the category, country music has reached deep into the heart of America's emotions and memories like no other sound. One indication of this—in 1991, 30 country music albums achieved gold or platinum status.

Country Stars Trivia

• Capital Records producer Allen Reynolds played a key role in Garth Brooks's success. He encouraged the talented entertainer to stop singing ballads in a full-voiced, operatic style and switch to a more natural, gentler manner. The successful ballads "If Tomorrow Never Comes" and "The Dance," Garth's signature hits, attest to Reynolds's insightful coaching.

• It's a rare occurrence on the Grand Ole Opry stage, but it happened in June 1987 when he made his first appearance: the audience applauded so enthusiastically that Ricky Van Shelton was called back for an encore.

• The late country singer Conway Twitty had one of the most outstanding careers in music history. He had 55 number-one hits, the most of any artist in any musical genre.

• Minnie Pearl said of this country artist, "A voice like his comes along once in a generation." He is Randy Travis.

• Wynonna Judd's solo career started off in a big way: "She Is His Only Need," her debut solo single, hit number 30 on the country singles chart of the 20-year-old trade newspaper *Radio and Records.* She's the first female performer to accomplish this.

• Who was the first female to win a country music Grammy? Dottie West.

• "I Want to Be a Cowboy's Sweetheart," recorded by Patsy Montana, became the first record by a female artist to sell over one million records.

• Merle Haggard has had 38 number-one country hits, more

Doug Stone

than Johnny Cash and Hank Williams combined.

• "The King of Western Swing" was bandleader Bob Wills, whose "Ahhaaa" hollers became his trademark.

• This Texas cowboy, in 1979, almost said good-bye to his music career, but his wife convinced him to stick it out for one more year. Eleven months later he signed with MCA. He now has 22 number-one hits under his belt, and all his albums are platinum or gold. With a stampede sellout at Madison Square Garden, he's "pure country" at its best— George Strait is his name.

• Chris LeDoux is not only a great country singer, he's also a famed western sculptor. His work has won first-place prizes at numerous art shows. Garth Brooks even owns one of Chris's works.

• At one time, pretty and talented Martina McBride sold T-shirts at Garth Brooks concerts.

Garth offered Martina the opening spot on his tour, giving her the start she needed.

• In 1989, Clint Black, who was born in New Jersey but grew up in Texas, was honored by the CMA as the winner of the coveted Horizon Award. This award is presented to the artist whose career has advanced the most in the past year.

• If Cleve Francis touches your heart with his songs, don't be surprised—he's also a practicing cardiologist.

• The vocal group Diamond Rio got the idea for the group's great name from the name of a truck that is manufactured in Pennsylvania.

• In 1991, Vince Gill became a member of the Grand Ole Opry. Besides having a great tenor voice, Vince is a good golfer.

• Opry member Marty Stuart is definitely the tops when it comes to "hillbilly fashion." He collects vintage country outfits (he currently has almost 200) that bring back that "hillbilly glitter" of the past. His album *This One's Gonna Hurt You* glitters too—it went gold.

• A. C. "Eck" Robertson was one of the first country musicians to wear full western apparel while singing country music during the 1920s.

• As of 1992, Reba McEntire and Wynonna Judd are the only two women in country music to have double-platinum studio albums—*For My Broken Heart* and *Wynonna,* respectively.

- In 1992, "Queen of Country Music" Reba McEntire was the first musical artist to have her entire concert broadcast live on the Jumbo-tron in Times Square from Radio City Music Hall in New York City.

- Singer Suzy Bogguss designs her own jewelry line and leather jackets for major department stores such as Macy's.

> ### Did Ya Know?
> Since 1944 over 14,000 country songs have been Top 40 country hits.

- "I Will Always Love You," a big hit by Whitney Houston, was written by Dolly Parton, who made it a number-one country hit in 1974.

- Ricky Van Shelton authored a children's book titled *Tales from a Duck Named Quacker.*

- Holly Dunn's heroes are Dale Evans and Roy Rogers. She's collected more than 300 items—from cap guns to comic books—from their colorful careers.

- The 13th-highest-paid entertainer in America during 1992 was Garth Brooks.

- Holly Dunn received two Grammy nominations for her song "Daddy's Hands," which was a present to her father for Father's Day. The song went on to become a gift to her fans also.

- In 1944, Chet Atkins failed an audition for Roy Acuff's band, but he went on to be one of the most popular and influential guitarists in the world.

The Jukebox

A uniquely American invention, the jukebox, popular during the 1930s and 1940s, has been around for more than a century. Wurlitzer, Rock-Ola, Seeburg, and AMI jukeboxes captivated everyone with their sights, bubbles, and sounds.

Country music played big on the jukebox, with 8 out of the 40 most-played jukebox singles of all time being country songs.

Originally, a jukebox could be purchased for about $250 and played only 12 records. They were named after "juke joints" (southern road houses), where they were quite popular.

Today, a thriving jukebox market exists, with the prettiest and rarest bubble makers selling for $30,000 and more. If Bubba shoots the jukebox, let's hope it's not one of these.

Nicknames & Titles of Country Stars

Johnny Cash

Stage names are not the only names some country stars go by. Many are known by their nicknames or titles as well. Nicknames can tell a fan something unique about the star. Sometimes a nickname is derived from a performer's most famous song, while another star's nickname may describe a personal trait or characteristic. Here are names that have "stuck" with some country stars over the years:

Roy Acuff
"The King of Country Music"

Bill Anderson
"Whispering Bill"

Eddy Arnold
"Tennessee Plowboy"

Carter Family
"First Family of Country Music"

Johnny Cash
"The Man in Black"

Little Jimmy Dickens
"Tater"

Merle Haggard
"Hag" or "The Stranger"

Tom T. Hall
"The Storyteller"

George Jones
"The Possum"

Loretta Lynn
"Coal Miner's Daughter"

Bill Monroe
"The Father of Bluegrass"

Jimmie Rodgers
"The Singing Brakeman"

Roy Rogers
"King of the Cowboys"

Ernest Tubb
"The Texas Troubadour"

Hank Williams, Jr.
"Bocephus"

Birthdays of Country Stars

John Anderson
December 13, 1954
Chet Atkins
June 20, 1924
Gene Autry
September 29, 1907
Moe Bandy
February 12, 1944
Clint Black
February 4, 1962
Garth Brooks
February 7, 1962
Kix Brooks
May 12, 1955
Johnny Cash
February 26, 1932
June Carter Cash
June 23, 1929
Rosanne Cash
May 24, 1955
Mark Chesnutt
September 6, 1963
Roy Clark
April 15, 1933
Billy Dean
April 2, 1962

Joe Diffie
December 28, 1968
Ronnie Dunn
June 1, 1953
Barbara Fairchild
November 12, 1950
Vince Gill
April 12, 1957
Merle Haggard
April 6, 1937
Emmylou Harris
April 2, 1947
Alan Jackson
October 17, 1958
George Jones
September 12, 1931
Wynonna Judd
May 30, 1964
Hal Ketchum
April 9, 1953
Brenda Lee
December 11, 1944
Patty Loveless
January 4, 1957
Barbara Mandrell
December 25, 1948

Kathy Mattea
June 21, 1959
Reba McEntire
March 28, 1955
Bill Monroe
September 13, 1911
Lorrie Morgan
June 27, 1959
Willie Nelson
April 30, 1933
Buck Owens
August 12, 1929
Dolly Parton
January 19, 1946
Eddie Rabbitt
November 27, 1941
Kenny Rogers
August 21, 1938
Ricky Skaggs
July 18, 1954
Doug Stone
June 19, 1956
George Strait
May 18, 1952
Marty Stuart
September 30, 1958

Pam Tillis
July 24, 1957
Randy Travis
May 4, 1959
Travis Tritt
February 9, 1963
Ernest Tubb
February 9, 1914
Tanya Tucker
October 10, 1958
Ricky Van Shelton
January 12, 1952
Porter Wagoner
August 12, 1930
Steve Wariner
December 25, 1954
Kitty Wells
August 30, 1919
Hank Williams, Jr.
May 26, 1949
Tammy Wynette
May 5, 1942
Trisha Yearwood
September 19, 1964
Dwight Yoakam
October 23, 1956

Fans always enjoy visiting the Country Music Hall of Fame.

Country Music Hall of Fame Members

The Country Music Hall of Fame was founded in 1961 by the Country Music Association and honors stars and music industry figures for their outstanding contributions to country music. The winners are announced each year at the CMA Awards show in October.

Jimmie Rodgers, 1961
Fred Rose, 1961
Hank Williams, 1961
Roy Acuff, 1962
Tex Ritter, 1964
Ernest Tubb, 1965
Eddy Arnold, 1966
James R. Denny, 1966
George D. Hay, 1966
Uncle Dave Macon, 1966
Red Foley, 1967
J. L. (Joe) Frank, 1967
Jim Reeves, 1967
Stephen H. Sholes, 1967
Bob Wills, 1968
Gene Autry, 1969
Bill Monroe, 1970
Original Carter Family, 1970
Arthur Edward Satherley, 1971
Jimmie H. Davis, 1972
Chet Atkins, 1973
Patsy Cline, 1973
Owen Bradley, 1974
Frank "Pee Wee" King, 1974
Minnie Pearl, 1975
Paul Cohen, 1976
Kitty Wells, 1976
Merle Travis, 1977
Grandpa Jones, 1978
Hubert Long, 1979
Hank Snow, 1979
Johnny Cash, 1980
Connie B. Gay, 1980
Original Sons of the Pioneers, 1980
Vernon Dalhart, 1981
Grant Turner, 1981
Lefty Frizzell, 1982
Roy Horton, 1982
Marty Robbins, 1982
Little Jimmy Dickens, 1983
Ralph Sylvester Peer, 1984
Floyd Tillman, 1984
Flatt and Scruggs, 1985
Benjamin F. Ford, 1986
Wesley H. Rose, 1986
Rod Brasfield, 1987
Loretta Lynn, 1988
Roy Rogers, 1988
Jack Stapp, 1989
Cliffie Stone, 1989
Hank Thompson, 1989
Tennessee Ernie Ford, 1990
Boudleaux & Felice Bryant, 1991
George Jones, 1992
Frances Williams Preston, 1992
Willie Nelson, 1993

Country Music Fan Fair

Country stars have a sincere "down-home" friendliness. No matter how big country singers become, they still put their fans first. Signing autographs and talking to the fans is as important as

being on the stage. Once a year the fans and the stars get the chance to meet at Fan Fair in Nashville, with more than 40 hours of music, autograph signing, and picture taking. This is an annual five-day extravaganza held at the Tennessee State Fair-grounds. For more information on the next Fan Fair, write: Fan Fair, 2804 Opryland Drive, Nashville, TN 37314, or call (615) 889-7503.

Fun and pictures with Steve Wariner at Fan Fair.

Fan Clubs

John Anderson
P.O. Box 810
Smithville, TN 37166
Clint Black
P.O. Box 299386
Houston, TX 77299
Suzy Bogguss
P.O. Box 7535
Marietta, GA 30065
Garth Brooks
c/o *Believers' Magazine*
P.O. Box 507
Goodlettsville, TN
37070
Brooks & Dunn
P.O. Box 24186
Nashville, TN 37202
Sawyer Brown
4219 Hillsboro Rd., #318
Nashville, TN 37215
Glen Campbell
10351 Santa Monica
Blvd., #300
Santa Monica, CA
90025

Mary-Chapin Carpenter
c/o Studio One Artists
7003 Carroll Ave.
Takoma Park, MD 20912
Carlene Carter
P.O. Box 120845
Nashville, TN 37212
Johnny Cash
Route 12, Box 350
Winston-Salem, NC
27107
Mark Chesnutt
P.O. Box 128031
Nashville, TN 37212
Mark Collie
P.O. Box 90132
Nashville, TN 37209
Billy Ray Cyrus
P.O. Box 121854
Nashville, TN 37212
Billy Dean
P.O. Box 23362
Nashville, TN 37202
Diamond Rio
P.O. Box 120261
Nashville, TN 37212

Joe Diffie
P.O. Box 479
Velma, OK 73091
Holly Dunn
P.O. Box 120964
Nashville, TN
37212
Cleve Francis
P.O. Box
15258
Alexandria,
VA 22309
Vince Gill
42 Music
Square West,
Suite 107
Nashville, TN
37203
Mickey Gilley
P.O. Box
1242
Pasadena, TX
77501

Lee Greenwood
1311 Elm Hill Pike
Nashville, TN 37210

Merle Haggard
P.O. Box 2065
Pinellas Park, FL 34664

Emmylou Harris
P.O. Box 99497
Louisville, KY 40299

Alan Jackson
P.O. Box 121945
Nashville, TN 37212

George Jones
Route 3, Box 150
Murphy, NC 28906

The Judds
P.O. Box 17325
Nashville, TN 37217

Hal Ketchum
P.O. Box 120205
Nashville, TN 37215

Tracy Lawrence
42 Music Square West,
110
Nashville, TN 37203

Chris LeDoux
P.O. Box 253
Sumner, IA 50674

Patty Loveless
42 Music Square West,
#11
Nashville, TN 37203

Loretta Lynn
P.O. Box 40328
Nashville, TN 37204

Barbara Mandrell
P.O. Box 800
Hendersonville, TN
37077

Kathy Mattea
P.O. Box 158482
Nashville, TN 37215

Martina McBride
68 Water St., Suite 406
Vancouver, BC Canada
V6B1A4

Reba McEntire
P.O. Box 121996
Nashville, TN 37212

Lorrie Morgan
P.O. Box 2204
Brentwood, TN 37027

Willie Nelson
P.O. Box 400
Wright, AR 72182

Dolly Parton
1020 Dollywood Lane
Pigeon Forge, TN 37863

Mike Reid
P.O. Box 218142
Nashville, TN 37221

Shenandoah
P.O. Box 2442
Muscle Shoals, AL
35662

Ricky Skaggs
P.O. Box 121799
Nashville, TN 37212

Doug Stone
P.O. Box 40465
Nashville, TN 37204

Pam Tillis
P.O. Box 25304
Nashville, TN 37202

Aaron Tippin
P.O. Box 121709
Nashville, TN 37212

Randy Travis
1604 16th Ave. South
Nashville, TN 37212

Travis Tritt
P.O. Box 440099
Kennesaw, GA 30144

Ricky Van Shelton
P.O. Box 120548
Nashville, TN 37212

Steve Wariner
P.O. Box 157
Nolensville, TN 37135

Trisha Yearwood
P.O. Box 65
Monticello, GA 31064

Billy Dean makes Fan Fair special for this young fan.

George Strait
P.O. Box 2119
Hendersonville, TN
37077

Marty Stuart
P.O. Box 1106
Tinley Park, IL 60477

**Sweethearts of the
Rodeo**
P.O. Box 160077
Nashville, TN 37216

Grand Ole Opry Members
2804 Opryland Drive
Nashville, TN 37214

If your favorite country
star's fan club isn't listed
here, write to **The Nashville Network**, Viewer
Services, 2806 Opryland
Drive, Nashville, TN
37214. They will send you
a complete listing.

The Instruments of Country Music

Country music couldn't exist without the musical instruments and the talented musicians that play them. Though not pictured, the piano, bass guitar, and drums are also used in country music. Here is a quick look at several prominent instruments that are heard over the country airwaves each day.

Five-String Banjo: The banjo and fiddle were the basic instrumental duo of the southern mountains in the 1700s. Originally banjos had only four strings, but in the 1830s a shorter fifth string was added. The banjo provided the rhythm for old-time music and dancing and was also used for playing melodies to complement old-time singing.

Did Ya Know?

Maybelle Carter developed a guitar technique in the 1920s that has been imitated by guitarists throughout recent history. Her method was to pick the melody with her thumb on the bass strings while her fingers brushed the treble strings for rhythm.

Pedal Steel Guitar: This Hawaiian instrument with its "crying sound" became very popular in mainstream country music in the 1940s.

Dobro: The dobro, a resonator guitar, was perfected by the Dopera Brothers of California, who introduced a single-resonator, wooden body style around 1928. Dobros produce a metallic, "jangly" sound. Roy Acuff, who made the dobro a distinctive feature in many of his recordings, popularized the instrument in America during the late '30s and early '40s.

Fiddle: When the violin appeared in the 16th century, it was rejected by serious composers. But rural folks found its music delightful for their energetic dancing. The fiddle was played at all political and social gatherings and became the defining instrument of country music. The first fiddling contest was held in 1736, and they are still popular in the South and Southwest. The sound of the fiddle thrills anyone with country music in their soul.

Guitar: The guitar is one of the most popular of contemporary instruments and can be used to play many different types of music, from folk songs and square-dancing tunes to country, jazz, and rock 'n' roll. It is equally at home as a rhythm or solo instrument. Though there are many varieties, there are two basic types of guitars: the acoustic (sometimes electrically amplified) and the electric guitar. The origin of the guitar is ancient and unknown. Some believe it may have come from Egypt.

Mandolin: This instrument came to America in the 1880s. It's a distant cousin of the guitar. Its popularity grew among rural Americans when mail-order catalogs, like those of Sears & Roebuck and Montgomery Ward's, began selling the instrument. The combination of the mandolin and guitar with vocal duets became very popular in country music during the 1920s.

Dulcimer: Considered a "solo instrument," the dulcimer is popular with folk musicians. It has a delicate sound and is most effective playing lonesome ballads and love songs.

Electric Guitar: The electric guitar was first used in country bands in 1934, when Bob Dunn played it with the Musical Brownies.

Places to Buy Instruments & Musical Instruction

Mountain Music Shop
109 N. Business 65, Branson, MO 65616 (417) 334-0515
Nationwide mail-order. Stop by and see these friendly folks when in Branson.

Gruhn Guitars Inc.
400 Broadway, Nashville, TN 37203 (615) 256-2033
New and vintage instruments. Catalog available.

Workshop Records
P.O. Box 49507, Austin, TX 78765 (512) 452-8348
This free catalog is a great source for video and cassette music instruction for bluegrass, country and more.

Harmonica: Sometimes called a mouth organ, this simple instrument was invented in the early 1800s. More harmonicas were brought to war from 1914 to 1918 than any other instrument in recorded history. It became very popular during America's early history because it could be easily obtained in country general stores and through the mail.

Country Stars Crossword Puzzle

This crossword puzzle is based upon the first number-one hit songs of 12 country stars. Fill in the stars' names. (Black squares separate first and last names.)

ACROSS

3. "Unwound," 1981
5. "Walk on Faith," 1991
6. "You May See Me Walkin'," 1981
7. "Delta Dawn," 1972
8. "(You Lift Me) Up to Heaven," 1980
9. "Why Baby Why," 1955
10. "A Better Man," 1989
11. "Dumb Blonde," 1967
12. "She's in Love with the Boy," 1991

DOWN

1. "Much Too Young," 1989
2. "Blue Blooded Woman," 1989
4. "When I Call Your Name," 1990

Answers: Across—3. George Strait; 5. Mike Reid; 6. Ricky Skaggs; 7. Tanya Tucker; 8. Reba McEntire; 9. George Jones; 10. Clint Black; 11. Dolly Parton; 12. Trisha Yearwood. Down—1. Garth Brooks; 2. Alan Jackson; 4. Vince Gill.

Chapter
7

WHERE TO
FIND THE
MUSIC

Dynamic Louise Mandrell thrills fans at the Grand Palace.

Branson

Branson, Missouri, had been the best-kept "hillbilly secret" in America until the national media began to focus its cameras on this small country community. Live country music from 27 theaters (and counting) draws millions of fans yearly to this country music mecca. What Aspen is to the skier, Branson is to the country music fan. This once-sleepy Ozark town is now making multimillion dollar deals. Over the past few decades, several hillbilly shows sprung up on the U.S. Highway 76 strip (now called "Country Music Boulevard" and "Entertainment Road"), the two most famous being the Baldknobbers and Presley's Mountain Music Jubilee. In 1983, Roy Clark came to town and since then other major country singers followed: Mel Tillis, Moe Bandy, Glen Campbell, and Louise Mandrell, just to name a few. Today, Branson is known as "America's Live Country Music Show Capital of the World," and rightly so. There are over 50,000 music-theater seats. Guaranteed, there will be more by the time you're reading this.

The Grand Palace, owned by Silver Dollar City and Kenny Rogers, is a spectacular state-of-the-art theater that seats 4,000. It is the largest theater in Branson (so far) and houses a recording studio and broadcast facilities. At the Grand Palace, hosted by Louise Mandrell and Glen Campbell, you'll be entertained by a galaxy of visiting stars such as Reba McEntire, Barbara Mandrell, Trisha Yearwood, Randy Travis, and many other first-class acts.

CITY LIMIT
BRANSON
POP. 3,706

Branson Theaters

Branson has such a variety of theaters that you will want to visit more than one show. It's entertainment the whole family can enjoy.

Andy Williams Moon River Theatre
2500 W. Highway 76
(417) 334-4500

The Baldknobbers Hillbilly Jamboree
2845 W. Highway 76
(417) 334-4528

The Boxcar Willie Theatre
3454 W. Highway 76
(800) 942-4626

The Braschler Quartet Music Show
310 Gretna
(417) 334-4363

The Buck Trent Dinner Theatre
S. Highway 165
(417) 335-5428

Campbell's Ozark Country Jubilee
3115 W. Highway 76
(800) 365-5833

Cedar Mountain Music Hall
W. Highway 76
Mutton Hollow
(417) 334-4947

Cristy Lane Theatre
3606 W. Highway 76
(417) 335-5111

Echo Hollow
Silver Dollar City
(417) 338-8118

The Foggy River Boys
2325 W. Highway 76
(417) 334-2563

The Grand Palace
2700 W. Highway 76
(417) 334-7263

Jim Stafford Theatre
3446 W. Highway 76
(800) 677-8533

Loretta Lynn Ozark Theatre
W. Highway 76
(417) 334-0023

Lowe's Country Music Theatre
3440 W. Highway 76
(417) 334-0428

Mel Tillis Theater
Highway 65 at
Highway 248
(417) 335-6635

Memory Lane Theatre
Branson Mall
W. Highway 76
(800) 477-5183

Mickey Gilley Theatre
3455 W. Highway 76
(800) 344-1936

Mel Tillis

Moe Bandy Americana Theatre
W. Highway 76
(800) 424-2334

Mutton Hollow Revue Dinner Theater
W. Highway 76
Mutton Hollow
(417) 334-4947

The Osmonds Theatre
W. Highway 76
(417) 336-6100

Ozark Mountain Amphitheater
Shepherd of the Hills
Expressway
(800) 765-4511

The elegant Grand Palace

Fans are always entertained by Glen Campbell at the Grand Palace.

Presley's Mountain Music Jubilee
2920 W. Highway 76
(417) 334-4874

Ray Stevens Theatre
3815 W. Highway 76
(417) 334-2422

Roy Clark Celebrity Theatre
3425 W. Highway 76
(417) 334-0076

76 Music Hall
1919 W. Highway 76
(417) 335-2484

Shoji Tabuchi Theatre
Shepherd of the Hills Expressway
(417) 334-7469

The Texans at Kirkwood Theatre
1825 W. Highway 76
(417) 334-0903

Wayne Newton Theatre
Shepherd of the Hills Expressway
(800) 759-2963

(Branson's zip code is 65616.)

Ticket Information

Branson Hotline
Complete information on concert tickets, hotels & lodging.
(800) 523-7589

Branson TIXS
(800) 888-TIXS

Chamber of Commerce
P.O. Box 220
Branson, MO 65616
(417) 334-4136
Enjoy your trip to Branson with the help of these friendly folks.

Branson Museums

Boxcar Willie Museum
3454 W. Highway 76
(417) 334-8656

Long's Wax & Historical Museum
3030 W. Highway 76
(417) 334-4145

Ralph Foster Museum
College of the Ozarks
Point Lookout, MO 65726
(417) 334-6411
Ext. 3407
"The Smithsonian of the Ozarks." Ozark heritage on display, a gun collection, plus the famed original Beverly Hillbillies car. Three miles from Branson.

The Rhinestone Cowboy Store & Museum
208 S. Commercial
(517) 335-4071
Downtown Branson.

See Moe Bandy live at the Moe Bandy Americana Theatre.

It's country music time at the Grand Ole Opry.

Nashville

"Music City USA" and "the Athens of the South" are names that describe this beautiful southern city surrounded by rolling woodlands and grassy meadows. This is "home" to country music—where the best studio musicians play for country's best singers. Where internationally televised country music shows are broadcast—while across town, on writer's night, an artist takes the mike and has a chance at stardom. In this town, country music can be seen on a stage or on the *General Jackson* showboat. It's the city many famous country entertainers call home.

Music City USA is an appropriate name—there are music publishers and recording studios everywhere. Nashville's recording studios are the envy of the world, with more gold and platinum than the United States government. Nashville could also be called a city of dreams, some fulfilled and some still waiting on tables.

One of the most famous landmarks is the Ryman Auditorium (formerly the home of Grand Ole Opry), also known as "the Mother Church of Country Music." It was from this simple wooden stage that the Opry's WSM radio performances were broadcast from 1943 to 1974. The Opry has since moved to newer, bigger surroundings with brighter lights, but the old Ryman is revered by many a country star who performed there during those magical years. Nashville is also home to Opryland USA, the Country Music Hall of Fame, "Ernest Tubb's Midnight Jamboree," Music Row, and many exciting museums.

Singers portraying country music stars in "Country Music U.S.A.," at Opryland.

Country Music in Nashville

"Ernest Tubb's Midnight Jamboree"
2414 Music Valley Dr. (37214)
(615) 889-2474
A live country music radio broadcast. It's free to the public.

General Jackson Showboat
2802 Opryland Drive (37214)
(615) 889-6611
Enjoy country music live in southern style on board this $12 million paddlewheel showboat.

Grand Ole Opry
2804 Opryland Dr. (37214)
(615) 889-3060

Every weekend, the nation's oldest radio show spotlights top country stars.

Nashville Chamber of Commerce
161 Fourth Ave. North Nashville, TN 37219
(615) 259-4700
These friendly people are always willing to help you find your way around Nashville.

The Nashville Network
2806 Opryland Dr. (37214)
(615) 883-7000
If you go to Nashville, don't miss the opportunity of seeing TNN's productions live. "Nashville Now" hosted by Ralph Emery, will cost $5.50. "Crook and Chase" and others are free.

Opryland USA
2802 Opryland Dr. (37214)
(615) 889-6700
A 120-acre "showpark," the world's only musical theme park. A must when visiting Nashville.

Nashville's Country Stars' Museums

These museums have mementos and treasured items of the stars. (All addresses are in Nashville unless otherwise noted.)

Barbara Mandrell Country
1510 Division St. (37203)
(615) 242-7800

Elvis Presley Museum
1520 Demonbreun St. (37203)
(615) 256-8311

Hank Williams, Jr. Museum
1524 Demonbreun St. (37202)
(615) 242-8313

House of Cash, Inc.
700 Johnny Cash Parkway
Hendersonville, TN 37075
(615) 824-5110

Jim Reeves Museum
1023 Joyce Lane (37216)
(615) 226-2065

Kitty Wells/Johnny Wright Family
240 Old Hickory Blvd.
Madison, TN (37115)
(615) 865-9118

Marty Robbins Memorial
2613A McGavock Pike (37214)
(615) 885-1515

Roy Acuff's Museum and Minnie Pearl's Museum
2802 Opryland Dr. (37214)
(615) 889-6700
Located in Opryland.

Twitty City
Music City Blvd.
Hendersonville, TN (37075)
(615) 822-6650

Other Country Music Hot Spots
Pigeon Forge, Tennessee
An action-packed family vacation spot.

Archie Campbell Theater
2775 Parkway (37863)
(615) 428-3218
Music and comedy.

Bonnie Lou & Buster's Smoky Mountain Hayride Show
3870 Parkway 37863
(615) 453-9590
Clogging, music, and comedy.

Music Mountain Amphitheater
2303 Parkway (37863)
(615) 428-3441
Enjoy country music in the outdoors.

Smoky Mountain Jubilee
Hwy. 441, on the Pkwy. (37863)
(615) 428-1836
Country, bluegrass, and gospel music.

Pigeon Forge Dept. of Tourism
P.O. Box 1390-G (37868)
(800) 251-9100 (outside Tennessee)
(615) 453-8574

Myrtle Beach Area
The country music center of the East Coast. Call (800) THE-OPRY for more information. This East Coast spot brings the beach and country music together.

The Carolina Opry
Myrtle Beach, SC

The Dixie Jubilee
N. Myrtle Beach, SC

Southern Country Nights
Surfside Beach, SC

Myrtle Beach Area Chamber of Commerce
1301 N. Kings Hwy.
Myrtle Beach, SC 29578
(803) 626-7444

More Hot Spots
Jamboree USA
1015 Main St.
Wheeling, WV 26003
(800) 624-5456
Saturday night country music in the Capitol Music Hall.

The Little Nashville Opry
Nashville, IN 47448
(812) 988-2235
Features country artists for the Midwest.

Renfro Valley Music Shows
Renfro Valley, KY 40473
(601) 256-2638
(800) 765-7464
Fun and country music in two show-barn theaters.

Did Ya Know?
A circular piece of the old wooden stage from the Ryman Auditorium (the home of the Grand Ole Opry from 1943 to 1974) was incorporated into the new Grand Ole Opry's stage in memory of all the country performers who performed there through the years.

Country Music Museums to Visit

Bob Wills Museum
Sixth and Lyles Streets
Turkey, TX
(806) 423-1033
The King of Western Swing is remembered with memorabilia of his colorful career. The Bob Wills Reunion, an annual event, is held on the last Saturday in April.

Country Music Hall of Fame and Museum
4 Music Square East
Nashville, TN 37203
(615) 256-1639
Where the history of country music comes alive, with over 3,000 artifacts ranging from costumes to rare instruments. See Elvis's gold Cadillac.

Country Music Wax Museum & Mall
118 16th Ave. S.
Nashville, TN 37203
(615) 256-2490
The world's first wax museum devoted to country music stars.

Grand Ole Opry Museum
2802 Opryland Drive
Nashville, TN 37214
(615) 889-6700
Don't miss the history of the Opry, with electronic displays and a video narrated by Porter Wagoner. Located in Opryland.

Music Valley Wax Museum of the Stars
2515 McGavock Pike
Nashville, TN 37214
(615) 883-3612
Over 50 lifelike wax figures of country music's stars, dressed in original costumes in natural settings. Plus the "Sidewalk of Stars," where more than 200 stars have placed their country footprints.

Music Village USA
44 Music Village Blvd.
Hendersonville, TN 37075
(615) 822-1800
Pick and choose from a variety of museums that showcase performers' personal items, costumes, and memorabilia from their music and movie careers. Check out the special events held in the l,700-seat theater.

Ryman Auditorium and Museum
116 Fifth Ave. N.
Nashville, TN 37219
(615) 254-1445
Home of the Grand Ole Opry from 1943 to 1974. A monument to the memories of country music legends, this world-renowned landmark is being renovated; fans will be thrilled to the sound of music here once again.

The Ryman Auditorium by Collect-A-Card (see page 89).

Musical Instrument Museums

The Grand Guitar
Highway 11 West
Bristol, TN 37620
(615) 968-1719
This museum has over 200 rare and unusual stringed instruments. Even the building is shaped like a guitar.

Miles Mountain Musical Museum
Highway 62 West
Eureka Springs, AR 72632
(501) 253-8961
Home to one of the largest and most unusual collections of musical instruments.

Chapter 8

COOKIN' WITH COUNTRY STARS

Recipes & Cookbooks

Country folk are known for their hospitality and down-home cookin'. The food is described as "finger lickin', lip smackin' good." Try some of these genuine mouth-waterin' recipes.

Branson's Country Music Cookbook

Memory Makers' Mud Cake & Icing

From the kitchen of Jana Henlebe, Diana Houseman, and Ami Leach.

1 cup margarine	1-1/2 cups flour
2 cups sugar	1-1/2 cups coconut
2 Tbsp. cocoa	1-1/2 cups nuts
4 eggs	1 jar marshmallow cream

In a large mixing bowl, combine margarine and sugar. Beat until fluffy. Add eggs and cocoa. Mix well. Add remaining ingredients, stirring well. Pour batter into greased and floured 13" x 9" baking pan and bake at 350° for 30 minutes.

Chocolate Icing

1 lb. powdered sugar	1/2 cup cocoa
1/2 cup margarine	1/2 tsp. vanilla
1/2 cup canned milk	

Combine all ingredients and mix until fluffy. Spread over cooled Mud Cake and serve to your favorite folks!

Mel Tillis' Corn Bread
(from scratch!)

1 Teflon skillet with lid	2 cups plain cornmeal
2 Tbsp. plain flour	2 tsp. baking powder
1 tsp. salt	1 tsp. baking soda

Combine these ingredients and mix thoroughly until all lumps are out.

1/4 cup cooking oil
2 cups buttermilk
1 egg

Combine and mix thoroughly. Preheat Teflon skillet on high 'til hot. Combine all ingredients in mixing bowl and mix 'til all ingredients are blended well. Pour into hot skillet and shake around until the batter is level. Put a lid on the skillet and turn burner down to low and let corn bread cook until done (about 20 min.). When done, turn corn bread over with an egg turner and let it brown on the other side. Don't put lid back on skillet while other side browns.

Louise Mandrell's Chicken and Dressing Casserole

1 4-lb. whole chicken	1–2 onions
3 stalks of celery	1 small carrot
1-1/2 tsp. salt	1 can cream of
1 can cream of	chicken soup
mushroom soup	1/4 cup cooking
1 12-oz. can evap-	sherry
orated milk	1 pkg. Pepperidge Farm herb
1/3 cup melted butter	stuffing mix

Put chicken and vegetables in large pot and cover with water. Add salt and bring to a boil. Cover and reduce to low. Cook 1 to 1-1/2 hours, until tender. Remove chicken to cool; debone and tear into small pieces. In food processor, puree onion, celery, and carrot with 1 cup of cooled broth.

In another saucepan, mix soups, sherry, milk, and pureed broth from the food processor together; heat slowly until warmed.

In a bowl, mix together stuffing and butter. Now we can begin to assemble casserole.

In a large 13" x 9" x 2" pyrex baking dish, which has been sprayed with Pam, pour 1 cup of soup mixture. Next, sprinkle 1/2 of stuffing/butter mixture evenly over soup. Next, layer 1/2 of the chicken pieces and 1/2 of of the remaining soup mixture. Repeat these layers starting again with the stuffing mix, remaining chicken, and remaining soup.

Optional: Finish by topping casserole with 3- or 4-ounce package of slivered almonds or cashews. Bake for 30 minutes or until bubbly in 325° oven. Serve with lots of cranberry sauce! Delicious! Serves 8.

Boxcar Willie's Broccoli Casserole

1 10-oz. pkg. broccoli	1 can cream of mushroom soup
1/2 can evaporated milk or	1 medium onion, chopped
regular milk	1 stick butter (1/2 cup)
1/2 lb. of Velveeta cheese	1-1/2 cups cooked rice
(diced or grated)	

Saute onion while butter is melting. Mix remaining ingredients together. Bake 1 hour at 350°.

Mickey Gilley's "Favorite Recipes"

Country Fried Chicken

1 fryer, cut up
1 cup flour
Salt and pepper

Cut up chicken; wash and drain. Salt and pepper all over. Roll into flour until well coated. Fry in deep Crisco until golden brown.

Mississippi Apple Cake

2 cups sugar	1 Tbsp. cinnamon
1 stick margarine	2-1/2 cups plain flour
2 eggs	1 cup buttermilk
1-1/4 tsp. soda	3 raw apples, chopped

Cream sugar and margarine; add eggs and beat well. Sift soda and cinnamon with flour. Add flour and buttermilk to creamed mixture. Last, add apples by folding. Bake in a greased tube pan at 325° for 50 or 60 minutes.

Did Ya Know?

The Indians of Mexico sundried thin strips of buffalo meat and called it *charqui*. For easy traveling, they would grind it into a mealy substance. When cooked in soup, it would swell and become a filling meal. The mountain men found it to be favorable, and later on the cowboys used beef instead of buffalo and named it "jerky."

Topping:

1/2 cup cream
1/2 tsp. vanilla
1 cup grated coconut
3 Tbsp. margarine
2/3 cup light brown sugar
1/2 cup chopped pecans

Cream sugar and margarine. Add cream, vanilla, coconut, and pecans. Spread over cake. Return to oven till sugar has melted.

Gone With the Grits
by Diane Pfeifer

Crispy Parmesan Squares

4 cups water
1 cup grits
1/2 teaspoon salt
1-1/2 cups Parmesan cheese

2 tablespoons flour
1/2 teaspoon seasoning salt
1/2 teaspoon pepper
Butter or oil for frying

Bring salted water to boil in medium saucepan. Slowly stir in grits. Cover, reduce heat, and cook, stirring occasionally until liquid is absorbed according to grits package directions. Stir in 1 cup Parmesan cheese.

Spread in 9" x 13" pan and let cool until firm. Cut into 2-inch squares.

Combine flour, seasoning salt, pepper, and remaining Parmesan cheese in medium bowl. Coat grits squares in breading mixture, turning until all sides are well coated.

Melt butter in large skillet. Fry grits until crispy on both sides.

Serves 6–8.

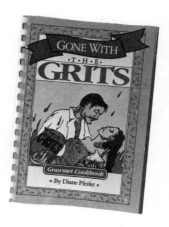

More Cookbooks

Taste the South and Southwest with these fine cookbooks, available at your local bookstore.

Cooking with Country Music Stars
by Anne Byrn

Country Desserts
by Lee Bailey

Cowboy Poetry Cookbook
by Cyd McMullen and Anne Wallace McMullen

Coyote Cafe
by Mark Miller

Farm House Cookbook
by Susan Herrmann Loomis

New Southern Cooking
by Nathalie Dupree

The New Texas Cusine
by Stephan Pyle

To Order Cookbooks

Branson's Country Music Cookbook and Mickey Gilley's "Favorite Recipes"
P.O. Box 357
Branson, MO 65616
(417) 334-6627

Branson's Country Music Cookbook is $10.00 plus $2 shipping. You'll get recipes from many Branson stars, including Louise Mandrell, Ray Stevens, and Roy Clark Celebrity Sound, to name a few. Pictures and information on the stars included. You'll love it!

Mickey Gilley's "Favorite Recipes" cookbook is $7.95 plus $2 shipping.

Gone with the Grits
by Diane Pfeifer
Published by
Strawberry Patch
P.O. Box 52404
Atlanta, GA 30355
(800) 875- 7242

A fun book with some unique ways to never run out of grits in your life. $9.95.

Mail-Order Vittles

Brazos Beef Emporium
700 S. Bryan St.
Bryan, TX 77803
(800) 8SAUCES
Free catalog. How could you go wrong with sauce names like these: "City Slicker Survival Kit," "Southern Hospitality Kit," and "The Prairie Fire."

Country Line "Air Ribs"
(800) 344-RIBS
Free brochure. Texas and barbecue are synonymous. If you can't go to this 1940s roadhouse-atmosphere restaurant, have your order air-mailed to you.

Jardine's Texas Foods
Texas Chili Fixin's
P.O. Box 160
Buda, TX 78610
(800) 544-1880
Free catalog. Award-winning chili works, salsa, and sauces.

John's Elgin Market
67 Fountain Square
Elgin, IL 60120
(708) 741-6374
The most exotic jerky available, including moose, elk, and buffalo.

Maurice's Gourmet Barbeque
P.O. Box 6847
W. Columbia, SC 29171
(800) MAURICE
Free brochure. Old South, pit-cooked, all-ham barbecue and mustard-based barbecue sauce.

New Braunfels Smokehouse
P.O. Box 311159
New Braunfels, TX 78131
(800) 537-6932
Free catalog. Quality hickory-smoked meats since 1945.

Grub Festivals

Brawley Cattle Call
Brawley Chamber of Commerce, Box 218
Brawley, CA 92227
(619) 344-3160
Chuck-wagon breakfast, rodeo, country music, and tons of fun. November.

East Texas Yamboree
221 Buffalo St.
Gilmer, TX 75644
(903) 843-2413
This festival "yams it up" with country music and a barn dance. October.

National Peanut Festival
169 Ross Clark Circle, S.E.
Dothan, AL 38301
(205) 793-4323
Honors the peanut farmer. Arts and crafts, hog show, and auto show. October.

Octoberfest and Carroll Country Pork Festival
P.O. Box 726
Huntingdon, TN 38344
(901) 986-4664
Celebrates fall and pork.

Prairie Dog Chili Cook-Off
Traders Village
2602 Mayfield Rd.
Grand Prairie, TX 75051
(214) 647-2331
Celebrates the "official state dish of Texas, chili." This one is done up big—rodeo, music, and dancing. April.

Strawberry Festival
P.O. Box 519
Tampa, FL 33601
(800) 826-8358
Parades, contest, music, and lots of strawberry shortcake. March.

World Grits Festival
St. George, SC
St. George is the "Grits Capital of the World."
(803) 563-3255
World Grits Olympics, grits parade, cooking contest, country and bluegrass music, and country western dancing. April.

Farming Museums

Agricultural Hall of Fame
630 N. 126th St.
Bonner Springs, KS 66012
(913) 721-1075

Luscher's Farm Relics of Yesterday
Manley Lustown Rd.
Frankfort, KY 40601
(502) 875-2755. Open after Memorial Day.

Chapter
9

ENTERTAINMENT

Kick Up Your Heels

Country entertainment is hotter than a two-dollar pistol. Dance clubs are kickin' up all over America. "Hillyuppies" are trading in their hectic lifestyles for a hat and boots. Traditional and simple fun, which has always been the "country way," is catching on with everyone from children to senior citizens.

Kickin' Kountry Dancers thrill the crowds with their excellent performances.

Country Western Dancing

Country western dancing is a fun way to catch the spirit of the West with popular dances such as the two-step, the waltz, the cowboy cha-cha, and the sweetheart schottische. These are based on Old World traditional dances such as the polka and schottische. It was in Texas and Oklahoma that the pioneers created the easy footwork and informal style of today's country western dances. The most popular, of course, is the two-step. It's a do-si-do that is smooth and moves counterclockwise around the outside of the dance floor. When you add the boots, hat, and

friendly smiles, you're guaranteed a foot stompin' good time.

Line dancing is all the rage these days and gives everyone the chance to dance without a partner. Some popular line dances are Tush Push, Electric Slide, the Achy Breaky, and the Boot Scootin' Boogie.

Square Dancing

Square dancing is associated with the rugged frontier of the West. In the 1930s, Lloyd "Pappy" Shaw, the father of western square dancing, popularized the dance throughout the country. His students from Cheyenne Mountain School in Colorado did so well with his dance program that they performed throughout America. His book, *Cowboy Dances*, published in 1939, quickly had American schools do-si-doin' and spreading the dance like wildfire.

Now there are over a million dancers and thousands of dance clubs in the United States, Canada, and 40 other countries. The National Square Dance Convention attracts 20,000 to 40,000 dancers each year. The Sands International Dance Festival, held in Las Vegas in December, includes square dancing, round dancing, clogging, country western dancing, and more. Square dancing has its own western duds for dolls and dudes. It gives a woman the excuse to buy pretty organdy petticoats, pettipants, and skirts to match her partner's western attire.

Square dancing, with its honor your partner, allemande left, grand right and left, and do paso, can be the hobby that baby boomers are looking for. Friendly and wholesome fun, square dancing will have you smiling as you learn to "slip the clutch," "box the gnat," and "shoot the star."

Cloggers performing at a jubilant Ozark festival.

Clogging

In the Appalachian Mountains it's common to hear phrases like "crazy legs," "eggbeater," and "possum trot" when you're involved in the dance called clogging. For this is the place that clogging has its roots and has been preserved. Clogging is time dancing, and the heels are the time keepers.

Clogging is one of the most original folk dances in America, yet its history has not been recorded. In the early days it was passed from one generation to another by watching others dance—it was "caught, not taught."

Whether clogging is done for competition or pure enjoyment, it always has these features—foot-stompin', hand clappin', and loud-shoutin' fun!

Hot Country Western Dances

Country dancing isn't new to instructors Darl and Regina Cameron of Kickin' Kountry Dancers, who have taught over 11,000 students traditional country western dancing in private and group lessons. They are the among the top 10 country western dance instructors in the world.

Closed Position
This position is for couple dancing and is used when more space is needed for lively dances.

Side-by-Side Position (Promenade)

Swing Position

The Two-Step

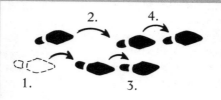

Did Ya Know?

Synchronization between partners, smoothness of motion, and keeping time with the music are the hallmarks of country western dancing.

Since it's the simplest country western dance to learn, the two-step is a good one to start with. Plus, it's the basis for many other dances. The couple dances counterclockwise around the outside of the floor. The man moves forward with his left foot, lifting the right heel, and the lady moves backward with her right foot, lifting her left toe. This is repeated for the last steps, but slower. The steps are "quick, quick, slow, slow." The two-step can be done to slow music or livened up for a country stomper.

The Country Western Waltz

The country western waltz is the romantic dance of western dancing. The step pattern is "long, short, short, long, short, short." Music is in 3/4 time, three beats to a measure. The waltz consists of gliding steps in which neither foot is ever lifted completely off the floor. Weight is kept on the balls of the feet with a smooth movement, keeping time with the rhythm and stepping on each beat of the music. The natural rise and fall of the body is accomplished by pushing with the hips. Start with the closed position. The man leads; the woman follows.

1. The man slides his left foot forward (long slide), as the woman slides her right foot back.

2. The man slides his right foot forward a short distance, so that the right heel is even with the left toe.

3. The man slides his left foot forward a short distance, so that the left heel is even with the right toe.

4. The man slides his right foot forward (long slide).

5. The man slides his left foot forward a short distance, so that the left heel is even with the right toe.

6. The man slides his right foot forward a short distance, so that the right heel is even with the left toe.

*Kickin'
Kountry
Dancers*

The Cowboy Boogie Line Dance

No partners are needed for line dancing. Kickers form straight lines. Dancers start with feet together and both hands resting in the waist area, such as thumbs in belt or pockets, or hands on hips.

Start.   1. Side right.   2. Cross left behind right.   3. Side right.   4. Kick left.   5. Side left.

6. Cross right behind left   7. Side left.   8. Kick right.   9. Forward right.   10. Kick left.   11. Forward left.

12. Kick right.   13. Step back right.   14. Step back left.   15. Step back right.   16. Kick left.   17–18. Rock forward left, twice.

      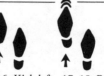

19–20. Rock back right, twice.   21. Rock forward left.   22. Rock back.   23. Step left, 1/4 turn.   24. Kick right.

Rules for Country Western Dancin'

• Smile at all times. It makes you look like you know what you're doing, even if you don't.

• With country western dancin', it's easy to get tangled up. So, in the beginning, don't be embarrassed if you look like a pretzel.

• Don't feel inhibited—yell out "Ee-haw" or "Ya-hoo" once in awhile to show you're having fun.

• There's a lot of spinnin' in country dancin', so practice at home. You don't want to develop "country nausea" on the dance floor.

• Remember to keep moving in the same direction as the rest of the kickers—most of them can move as fast as a hound on fresh tracks.

• If you're dancin' on a crowded floor, take small steps and keep your eyes open and watch in all directions. This will prevent "brim collision."

• It's a good idea not to dance above the level of your partner—especially if you want to go home with all 10 toes.

• Country western dancin' gives you a chance to be a cowboy or cowgirl, so don't show up without your duds on.

Dance Information

Country Dance Lines Magazine
Drawer 139
Woodacre, CA 94973
(415) 488-0154
A must for country western dancers; news, views, and dance instructions. $18 a year.

National Square Dance Directory
P.O. Box 880
Brandon, MS 39043
(800) 542-4010 (orders only)
(601) 825-6831
Over 10,000 square, round, contra, clogging, and folk dance clubs throughout the world. Lists festivals, conventions, and other useful information. $12.

Country Western Dance Floor

Outside Edge: Progressive Dancers

Inside: Stop & Go Dancers

Center: Line or Swing Dancers

119

Famous Lines from Famous Western Movies

If you saw these western movies, do you remember what candy bar or what kind of popcorn—plain or buttered—you were eating when these words were spoken?

Famous Line	Western Movie
"The larceny of an equine is a capital offense, but a horse thief always gets a fair trial before he's hung."	*The Westerner*
"I call that bold talk for a one-eyed fat man!"	*True Grit*
"I knowed General George Armstrong Custer for what he was. . . ."	*Little Big Man*
"To talk peace is not hard. To live it is very hard."	*Broken Arrow*
"I didn't know who you were when I said you were cheating."	*Butch Cassidy and the Sundance Kid*
"The pay is $13 a month. The diet—beans and eggs. Maybe horse meat before this campaign is over. They fight over cards or rotgut whiskey, but share the last drop in their canteens."	*Fort Apache*
"The specialty of the house and it's still moving."	*Butch Cassidy and the Sundance Kid*
"It's no good. I've got to go back. They're making me run. I've never run from anybody before."	*High Noon*
"I can't rightly say any place is my home—I belong where I am!"	*The Man from Laramie*
"All gunfighters are lonely. They live alone and they die without a dime, a woman, or a friend."	*Gunfight at the O.K. Corral*
"If you want to call me that—smile!"	*The Virginian*
"There's gold in them thar hills."	*Blue Steel*
"Cowboying is something you do when you can't do nothin' else."	*The Culpepper Cattle Co.*
"I think we lost 'em! Do you think we lost 'em? . . . neither do I!"	*Butch Cassidy and the Sundance Kid*

Classic Western Videos to Rent

Western movies are uniquely American, for they were born in the minds and hearts of Americans. The terrain, the town, the people on Main Street—all are American. Viewing a western movie is like viewing a slice of

John Wayne

our history. Whether real or imagined (suspicions are that the latter is more accurate), the Old West is vividly encapsulated on celluloid for young and old to enjoy. There's a little of the Old West—independence, adventure, freedom—in all of us. Maybe that's the reason the myths of the Old West continue to live on.

Bite the Bullet
This epic adventure concerns a 600-mile horse race. Gene Hackman and James Coburn star.

Butch Cassidy and the Sundance Kid
Paul Newman and Robert Redford skillfully combine action with comedy in this gentle western spoof.

The Cowboys
The Duke (John Wayne) is a rancher who must get his cattle to market, but his wranglers have been taken with gold fever, so he's forced to hire some greenhorns.

Dark Command
Once again the Duke (Wayne) has to set things straight when a once-honest man goes renegade, with help from Roy Rogers and Gabby Hayes.

Dodge City
Errol Flynn, with an all-star cast, sets out to clean up and tame the wild city of Dodge.

El Dorado
John Wayne and Robert Mitchum star in this tale of a land war.

Gunfight at the O.K. Corral
Burt Lancaster and Kirk Douglas portray gunfighters in 1881 Tombstone, Arizona, who shoot it out with the Clanton family.

High Noon
It's the sheriff's (played by Oscar-winner Gary Cooper) wedding day, but the head of an outlaw gang has promised vengeance against him at noon. The townspeople desert the sheriff as the clock ticks closer to the dreaded hour.

The Man from Laramie
James Stewart's finest western performance, as a stranger quarreling with an influential and powerful ranching family.

Red River
John Wayne is featured as a tough rancher making a historic cattle drive.

Shane
A mysterious stranger, played by Alan Ladd, helps a group of homesteaders as they struggle with a group of cattlemen. One of the best westerns ever made.

Hollywood & Western Trivia

Q. What was the name of the first Zane Grey western novel to be made into a movie?
A. *Fighting Blood*, made in 1911.

Q. What actor of the silent screen grew so fond of his movie horse that he acted in a movie free of charge to own the horse?
A. William S. Hart. Hart estimated it cost him $40,000 for his horse Fritz.

Q. What was John Wayne's first movie role as a leading man in Hollywood?
A. *The Big Trail*, released in 1930. Wayne played Brick Coleman, a wagon-train scout.

Q. What was the name of the movie that made Gene Autry a nationally known "singing cowboy" star?
A. *Tumbling Tumbleweeds*, in 1935.

Q. What two things were responsible for creating the western sagas?
A. The "dime novels" and the Wild West shows. Americans were hungry for a glorious past, and the legends of the West, through books and the Wild West shows, fulfilled this need in the late 1800s.

Q. Who first filmed *The Great Train Robbery,* and how long did it take?
A. It took Edwin S. Porter (Thomas Edison's assistant) two days.

Q. What was John Wayne's real name?

Roy Rogers and Trigger

A. Marion Morrison—he was given the name John Wayne by film director Raoul.

Q. How did David Horsely affect the film industry's vision of the West?
A. In 1911, David Horsely's Nestor Films was the first film company to establish its studio in Hollywood. The wisdom of the move was readily apparent, with western scenery everywhere. Soon other film companies did likewise, and the American film industry, once based in New York, shifted to Hollywood.

Q. What western movie recounted Oklahoma's history and was the first western to win an Academy Award for best picture of the year?
A. *Cimarron,* in 1931.

Q. What country singer and actor sang the Academy-Award-winning ballad "High Noon"?

A. Singing cowboy Tex Ritter, who made 65 movies in his career.

Q. How long did it usually take to film one of the Roy Rogers and Gene Autry movies of the 1930s?
A. About a week.

Q. Who is considered to be the most popular woman in the history of westerns?
A. Dale Evans.

Q. What remark did director John Ford make about John Wayne after he saw the movie *Red River?*
A. "I didn't know the big lug could act."

Q. What actor was working as a common laborer to supplement his income when, one day, while waiting for a friend at CBS to go out for lunch, an executive producer asked if he was an actor? Because he had all the physical attributes and the personality the producer was looking for, he was tested and promptly signed for a TV series that became an instant success.
A. Clint Eastwood (he was signed for the part of Rowdy Yates in "Rawhide").

Q. Who played young George Armstrong Custer in *The Santa Fe Trail,* a 1940 western tale?
A. Ronald Reagan.

Q. Why was *Stagecoach* such an important movie for John Wayne, and what character did he play?

A. Directed by John Ford and released in 1939, *Stagecoach* was considered to be a masterpiece, and it was John Wayne's first big starring vehicle. Wayne played the Ringo Kid.

Q. What was the name of the first full-fledged western movie, and where was it filmed?
A. *The Great Train Robbery.* When the movie was first viewed by the American audience in 1903, people screamed and fainted, and demanded that the movie be shown again and again. It was shot on location near Dover, New Jersey, and became the father of all westerns.

Q. Why was the 1930 western *The Indians Are Coming* such an important movie?
A. It included dialogue in Sioux and became the first western film to use American Indian language on screen.

Q. What three Italian-made Westerns did Clint Eastwood star in, and how did they change his career?
A. Eastwood quickly went from being a TV supporting actor to an international film star after starring in the Italian films *A Fistful of Dollars, For a Few Dollars More,* and *The Good, the Bad, and the Ugly.*

Your TV & Radio Guide

Cable Networks

Americana Television Network, Inc: "The music, people, and pastimes of this great nation" and what's hot in Branson. (417) 335-8600

CMT (Country Music Television): "All day. All night. All video."

TNN: With over 60 million subscribers, and only 10 years old, this cable network reaches 93 percent of all cable households in the United States. It's definitely the heart of country and will keep you informed on the latest about your favorite stars.

Several TNN Programs

Be A Star: Talent contest.

Club Dance: Hosted by Shelley Magrum. Great country dancin'.

Cookin' USA: Hosted by Merle Ellis. Unique recipes and cookbooks featured.

Country Kitchen: Hosted by Florence Henderson. Kitchen fun with Florence and the stars.

Crook & Chase: Hosted by Lorianne Crook and

Crook and Chase

Charlie Chase, a good lookin' duo of Nashville insiders who have the scoop on who's hot and what's new. Movie reviews, country news, and star interviews.

Grand Ole Opry Live: Country at its *best*. As American as apple pie.

Nashville Now: Host Ralph Emery shines in interesting conversations with country stars. Plus, see Shotgun Red.

Miller & Company: Talk show.

On Stage: Concert series of country stars.

Video Morning: Hot country videos with hosts Al Wyntor & Katie Haas.

Video PM: Country music videos.

"Watch country 'til you drop."

Country Radio Stations

Here's a partial listing of the many excellent stations you can listen to:

Anchorage, AK **KASH 107.5**	Duluth, MN **WAVC 105.1**	Pendleton, OR **WKHT 103.5**
Atlanta, GA **WKHX 590**	Fort Worth, TX **KSCS 96.3**	Phoenix, AZ **KMLE 107.9**
Baltimore, MD **WCAO 600**	Greenville, SC **WESC 92.5**	Pittsburgh, PA **WDSY 107.9**
Bangor, ME **WYOU 97.1**	Hartford, CT **WWYZ 92.5**	Providence, RI **WHIM 550**
Bellevue, WA **KBLV 1540**	Houston, TX **KIKK 95.7**	Reno, NV **KBUL 98.1**
Billings, MT **KCTR 103**	Jackson, MS **WMSI 102.9**	Richmond, VA **WKHK 95.3**
Birmingham, AL **WVOK 690**	Lafayette, LA **KMDL 97.3**	Roswell, NM **KRSY 1230**
Boise, ID **KGEM 1140**	Little Rock, AR **KSSN 95.7**	Sacramento, CA **KRAK 1140**
Boonville, IN **WBNL 1540**	Louisville, KY **WAMZ 97.5**	Seattle, WA **KMPS 1300**
Branson, MO **KRZK 106.3**	Lowell, MA **WLLH 1400**	Sioux Falls, SD **KXRB 1000**
Cedar Falls, IA **KCFI 1250**	Madison, WI **WWQM 106.3**	Springfield, MO **KTTS 94.7**
Charleston, WV **WQBE 97.5**	Nashville, TN **WSM 650**	Topeka, KS **KTPK 106.9**
Charlotte, NC **WSOC 103.7**	New York, NY **WYNY 103.5**	Trenton, NJ **WTTM 920**
Cheyenne, WY **KUUY 650**	Norfolk, VA **WSKX 106.9**	Wausau, WI **WDEZ 101.9**
Chicago, IL **WUSN 99.5**	Oklahoma City, OK **KXXY 1340**	Wheeling, VW **WOKV 98.7**
Columbus, OH **WMNI 920**	Orlando, FL **WWKA 92.3**	Waikahu, HI **KDEO 940**
Denver, CO **KXKL 1280**		
Detroit, MI **WWWW 106.7**		
Dover, DE **WDSD 94.7**		
Dover, NH **WOKQ 97.5**		

Did Ya Know?

The number of country music stations in the United States has exploded from 1,500 in 1980 to 2,500 in 1992.

Keeping Informed: Magazines & Books

With the momentum and position country music and the western lifestyle have gained in today's world, it's easy to keep informed. There are plenty of books and magazines out there to do the job. Here is a list that will help you.

Magazines

Branson's Country Review
P.O. Box 357
Branson, MO 65616
(417) 334-6627
Branson's entertainment magazine. $10.97 for a one-year subscription.

Country America
P.O. Box 10830
Des Moines, IA 50336
(800) 374-8739
"The magazine of country life and entertainment." One of the best.

Country Music
329 Riverside Avenue
Westport, CT 06880
(203) 222-5800
A favorite of country fans for over 20 years.

Country Sampler's WEST
P.O. Box 7300
Red Oak, IA 51591
(800) 666-2255
"The spirit of the frontier home."

Country Song Roundup
40 Violet Avenue
Puughkeepsie, NY 12601
(914) 454-7420
Lyrics to the popular country songs and interviews with country stars.

Cowboy Magazine
P.O. Box 126
La Veta, CO 81055
(719) 742-5250
"For People Who Value the Cowboy Lifestyle."

Music City News
50 Music Square West
Nashville, TN 37203
(615) 329-2200
Lots of information for country music fans.

Singing News
727B Blowing Rock Road
Boone, N C 28607
(704) 264-3700
Southern gospel music's voice.

Western Styles
P.O. Box 369
Mount Morris, IL 61054
(800) 877-5278
Beautiful photography of western fashions and the best of the West.

Yippy Yi Yea
8393 E. Holly
Holly, MI
(800) 437-1218
A great magazine with decorating, gifts, and western articles.

Books

Find out more about country music and your favorite stars with the following books—available at your local bookstore.

The Country Music Message: Revisted
by Jimmie N. Rogers
A good one for country music newcomers.

Country Music, U.S.A.
by Bill C. Malone
Everything you've ever wanted to know about the history of country music.

Garth Brooks: Platinum Cowboy
by Edward Morris

Get to the Heart: My Story, Barbara Mandrell
by Barbara Mandrell with George Vecsey

The Judds
by Bob Millard

Memories
by Ralph Emery
An autobiography about this legendary country music talk-show host.

Randy Travis: King of Country Traditionalists
by Don Cusic

Reba: Country's Music Queen
by Don Cusic

Country Festivals

Family fun at Silver Dollar City.

Festivals are a great place to see country shine. There's always plenty of homespun fun, dancing, music, and food.

Azalea Festival
Chamber of Commerce
Muskogee, OK 74401
(918) 682-2401
Celebrates in the 100-acre Honor Heights Park with music, rodeo, chili cookoff, and thousands of Azaleas in bloom. April.

Fine Arts Festival
Calico Ghost Town
P.O. Box 638
Yermo, CA 92398
(619) 254-2122
Western art, country and bluegrass music. November.

Mountain Dance and Folk Festival
Asheville, NC
Dance teams, bluegrass music, old-time fiddlers.
(800) 257-1300
August.

Mountain Festival
P.O. Box 401
Tehachapi, CA 93561
(805) 822-4180
Country western dancing, PRCA rodeo, arts and crafts. August.

Ozarks Heritage Reunion
Rt.3
Fair Grove, MO 65648
(417) 759-7503
Music, dancing, clogging, food, and crafts in this authentic mill town—it's great. September.

Roan Mountain Rhododendron Festival
P.O. Box 190
Elizabethton, TN 37643
(615) 543-2122
Six-hundred acres of flowers, mountain cloggers, and music. June.

War Eagle Annual Fair
Ozarks Arts & Crafts
P.O. Box 1577
War Eagle Farms
Hindsville, AR 72738
(501) 789-5343
This huge arts and crafts show is a must. October.

World Championship Cowchip Throwing Contest
Beaver Chamber of Commerce
P.O. Box 878
Beaver, OK 73932
(405) 625-4726
Wild West shoot-out, country music, and, of course, a cowchip throwing contest. April.

Yellow Daisy Festival
P.O. Box 778
Stone Mountain, GA
30086 (404) 498-5637
Music, arts and crafts, dancing and hog calling contest. September.

Take a stagecoach ride during Ozarks Heritage Reunion.

Theme Parks

Dollywood
700 Dollywood Lane
Pigeon Forge, TN 37863
(800) DOLLYWOOD
National Crafts Festival and a lot of country fun and music.

Fiesta Texas
San Antonio, TX 78257
200 acres of music shows, rides, and Texas culture.
(800) IS-FIESTA

Opryland USA
(See page 104.)

Silver Dollar City
Branson, MO 65616
(417) 338-8211
This turn-of-the-century-theme park is a must when visiting Branson. Music, rides, and crafts.

Chuck-Wagon Suppers & Western Shows

"A taste of the West!" These cowboys know how to cook and entertain you. Bring the buckaroos and enjoy the spirit of the West. Call for a brochure and to make reservations.

Bar-J Ranch
P.O. Box 220
Wilson, WY 83014
(307) 733-3370

Circle B
HC 33
Box 3611
Rapid City, SD 57702
(605) 348-7358

Lazy B Ranch
P.O. Box 130
Estes Park, Colorado
80517
(303) 586-5371

Index

B

Index

B